A *New* Program

This book was produced over
three days in Los Angeles,
based on eight years of teaching at Princeton University.
One semester-long course
was compressed and presented
each day as six 45-minute
lectures. These were recorded,
transcribed, and edited with
additional post-production.

for Graphic Design

David Reinfurt

INVENTORY PRESS

D.A.P./Distributed Art Publishers

**Preface
Adam Michaels**

Something I learned today / Black and white is always grey
Looking thru the window pane / I'm not inside your brain
Something I learned today / Yield to the right-of-way
Stopping at a 4-way sign / Someone else's rules, not mine
Something I learned today / Never look straight in the sun's rays
Letting all the sunshine in / Can't remember where I've been
—Hüsker Dü, "Something I Learned Today," *Zen Arcade*

Power cannot be divided up. There is only one power, that of saying
and speaking, of paying attention to what one sees and says. One learns
sentences and more sentences; one discovers facts, that is, relations
between things, and still other relations that are all of the same nature;
one learns to combine letters, words, sentences, ideas.... This is what
everything is in everything means: the tautology of power. All the power
of language is in the totality of a book. All knowledge of oneself as an
intelligence is in the mastery of a book, a chapter, a sentence, a word.
—Jacques Rancière, *The Ignorant Schoolmaster*

It all began straightforwardly enough: A conversation on Manhattan's
Lower East Side in late 2016, during which it became clear that the
condensed graphic design curriculum that David Reinfurt had been
teaching at Princeton University for several years could be of use
to a more widespread audience, far beyond that bucolic campus in
New Jersey. It struck me that a book—this book—could help fill a void
in the educational literature for a relentlessly shifting design field.

David's curriculum is built upon a range of propositions; perhaps
most significantly, based on the observation that graphic design
is everywhere, encompassing the means through which most written
language is transmitted, it follows that a heightened understanding
of the means and messages of graphic design should ideally be part of
every general education, taught in tandem with other language skills.
Teaching from this premise within the setting of a large university—not
an art or design school—David was able to test and expand upon the
proposition, working with students across a range of backgrounds, interests, majors, and intended career paths, receiving feedback throughout
the process.

As we discussed the notion of developing a book based on the
program and its three courses (Typography, Gestalt, and Interface),
David was quickly enthusiastic, while nearly as rapid to identify the
difficulty and the questionable appropriateness of setting out to write

a conventional book as an outgrowth from a decidedly unconventional, albeit pragmatic, program.

Seeing this as an opportunity rather than a problem (so to speak), a range of long-standing mutual obsessions came to mind: feats of absurd educational endurance such as Buckminster Fuller's 42-hour lecture "Everything I Know" and Michael Asher's legendary marathon CalArts critiques; books like William James' *Pragmatism: A New Name for Some Old Ways of Thinking*, composed of a series of lectures delivered in 1906 and 1907; and John Berger's *Ways of Seeing*, based on his 1972 BBC television series.

In short, it became apparent that the most natural way for David to write/ not write the book, would be to speak the book. We determined that each semester-length course could correspond to a day of six 45-minute lectures, with the compressed semesters then being presented over three consecutive days. And as this subject matter had only been presented in real time to successive groups of students in a classroom setting, it followed that an audience ought to be assembled (and encouraged to provide feedback)—though at a deliberate remove from the familiar Princeton setting.

Fortuitously, we had access to an ideal site for our purposes: Richard Neutra's former studio in the Silver Lake section of Los Angeles, designed by the architect in 1950, and where Inventory Press and IN-FO.CO were then based. It was exceptionally fitting for our events to take place in this setting, with its layers of design history on immediate display. In bringing together our audience, we reached out to various Los Angeles educators, designers, and others; we were thrilled to be joined by an engaged group for all three days.

The *new* program began on the morning of Friday, July 13, 2018. It was an anxious moment for all—was it a ridiculously wrongheaded idea to think that a year-and-a-half of teaching could be compressed into three very long days? Was it physically possible or generally advisable for one person to speak at such a length? Happily, the condensed curriculum was well-received, and David's voice only gave out on Sunday, with a large quantity of apple, lemon, and ginger juice enabling him to push through to the end of the day.

The days were densely informational, but also genuinely festive, with a strong sense of play running throughout. Each 45-minute lecture was followed by a 15-minute break; each break featured a crudely programmed, vaguely PBS-inspired theme song played on synthesizers with their parameters altered each time based on the mood of the room (tranquil, then perky in the morning; sluggish, then alert after lunch; fatigued yet determined toward the end of the day). Friends and collaborators brought in other sound and video gear, adding an unexpectedly appropriate demonstration of a variety of interface designs. Food and drink (especially coffee) were available for the audience throughout the three days, and a reading room (as well as the nearby Silver Lake Meadow park) provided space for needed breaks. The main space was further filled out by wallpaper featuring a loose composition of nearly all of the lecture images—which, in turn, now form the foundation of this book's illustrations—in addition to a digitally projected exhibition of student work spanning all of David's years teaching at Princeton.

The three days were well-documented as audio and video, and shortly after the events had concluded, we set to work on a transcript, which formed the first (very) rough draft of this book. This was an invaluable starting point, and also when we realized just how much further editing and writing would be necessary in order to present the spoken lectures here in print. So while this book isn't strictly a verbatim transcript of our three days in Los Angeles, the spirit and tone appears to have emerged intact, with an unconventional process leading to the desired outcome of an unconventional book—one that we hope the reader finds to be a genuinely useful resource in their own ongoing investigations.

Foreword
Ellen Lupton

When I started reading the early page proofs of this book, I expected to learn how to do graphic design. I thought I would be revisiting the rules of typography and examining how basic forms build complex meanings. I expected a textbook. Instead, I found a curious history of visual communication. I learned where the science of visual perception came from and how it influenced a generation of technology-minded modernists. I learned how Muriel Cooper, co-founder of MIT's Visible Language Workshop, forged new relationships between author and designer, reader and writer. I traced the history of a clock face from a piazza in Venice to the Apple watch.

In this book, you will meet all kinds of people: writers, printers, scientists, and industrialists. Most of these characters arrive from outside the familiar story of graphic design. These generalists see graphic design as a tool for publishing, a way of seeing, or a branch on a tree. Benjamin Franklin, before he became a "founding father" of America's endangered democracy, was a printer and typographer. Indeed, he used his design skills to agitate for revolution. He was successful at business, and graphic design served him well there, too. He came of age in his brother's printshop, which published a drumbeat of political pamphlets alongside the first independent colonial newspaper. Learning to be a printer inspired Franklin to become a writer. The physical craft precipitated the intellectual one. I write because I design.

Many of the intellectual generalists you will meet in this book wrote books of their own. *A Primer of Visual Literacy*, written by Donis A. Dondis in 1973, claims that optimized perception is the basis of abstract design principles. Her book builds on the work of other people you'll meet in this one, including Muriel Cooper, Max Wertheimer, György Kepes, and Rudolf Arnheim (pioneers and practitioners of Gestalt psychology). We also get to know Reinfurt, whose own creative work speaks to each of these histories. Reinfurt is an experimental designer, artist, writer, and publisher. He is also an educator. *A *New* Program for Graphic Design* is based on a course he teaches in the Program in Visual Arts at Princeton University. Reinfurt approaches graphic design as a liberal art—"a body of knowledge to collect or assemble, which informs everything else you think about."

Graphic design certainly informs everything I think about. Each word I type on a screen or scratch in a notebook is an embodied, material figure destined to convey ideas to a future self or to a reader, known or unknown. Graphic design is the infrastructure of history. ("Give me twenty-six lead soldiers," Franklin is credited with saying, "and I will conquer the world.") People empowered to access marks, symbols, and scripts are those who have written history, creating the corpus of official culture and its counterpoints of protest and samizdat. Graphic design, in its generality as a liberal art, harbors endless links between the tools of communication and the history of thought and action.

Reinfurt compares reading Dondis' *Primer of Visual Literacy* to "sitting in a classroom, in a good way." The same holds true for Reinfurt's book. He speaks to us from a design studio in Los Angeles, where he is reading text out loud, based on lectures delivered some time earlier to students at Princeton. This transcribed performance has been edited with a light touch, preserving a tone both erudite and at ease.

The book stands as a manifesto for making books. This book is a portable device connecting us to a network of friends and influencers. It has a relaxed, friendly interface and a non-invasive service plan. It doesn't cost much, and it won't weigh you down. It is the same trim size as Dondis' *Primer* (6 × 9 inches) and has a similar layout: a single column of sans serif text punctuated by diagrams and pictures, like slides in a lecture. In 1973, Dondis' book cost $6.95. It's still in print, selling today for $34—pricey for a paperback, but hardly a scam.

But textbooks can be a scam. Official textbook publishers occupy a specialized, highly lucrative branch of the book industry. In 2018, college students in the U.S. spent an average of $1,200 a year on textbooks and course materials. Pearson Education, the largest textbook publisher in the U.S., sells a typography primer similar in size to this book for over $75.

This, however, is not a conventional textbook, either in its form or its method of distribution. A typical textbook is stocked with methods and rules. It presents canonical knowledge about an established field of study—such as heart surgery or conversational French. This book is not canonical, and its field of study—graphic design—is not established. Reinfurt weaves a personal path through an infinite history. He shows us different ways individuals have used typography, publishing, and manufacturing to author their own ideas. He seeks out places where art, design, and science meet. Countless other paths and intersections are possible. Yours might be more ornamental, political, or postcolonial.

This book is a manifesto for graphic design. It takes a broad view of design's outcomes—from a pamphlet, road sign, or typeface to a diagram, interface, or kinetic sculpture. By putting "graphic design" in the title of his book, Reinfurt shows love for a fuzzy, ubiquitous practice that often seems to be coming and going at the same time. The profession of graphic design is both young (just a century old) and a target for nostalgia in a technocratic culture focused on "user experience" and "innovation." Graphic design joins thinking and making. It embraces craft, complexity, and play. Like Reinfurt himself, many of the polymaths profiled in this book don't self-identify strictly as graphic designers. Many readers of this book won't either, but anyone interested in spreading ideas can find a way in.

Introduction

This is an experiment—that's the first thing to know. And everybody here is part of it. It's maybe a harebrained idea to perform a book rather than write one, but here it is. Each of the next three days will cover one of my graphic design courses at Princeton University, delivered as a consecutive series of slide lectures. All of this will be video-recorded and transcribed to form the basis of a new publication, so that what's said here now is also writing a book elsewhere in the future.

Histories, and figures from them, bleed from one course to the next, alongside some of my own work. This is both by design and a practical consideration. When taking courses I always liked to know where the teacher was coming from so that I had some idea of how to orient myself. This won't be a laundry list of—or "how to do"—graphic design, but rather an attempt to provide a few models of how others have practiced design before. These are models I like. Or that I know about. Or that I've found particularly rich for students. Sometimes these are stories I have stumbled on and followed my instincts toward (or, less generously, indulged my impulses for). It is barely a partial account, entirely idiosyncratic, pragmatic, and ad hoc. I've very often found when teaching that it works better when you model a behavior rather than demonstrate or instruct it. And, so, I hope by suggesting some exemplary practices from the past and knitting those together, as well as collecting examples that might be outside of the scope of what we immediately think of as graphic design, then that also indicates a kind of approach. These interests, cultivated, are what get a design practice moving, and keep it moving. I feel like today you need a solid bit of internal ballast to go against all the forces that want you to operate within a very narrow band. There's just no need to be so limited—there are lots of opportunities— and many new ways—to work as a graphic designer, particularly now.

Eight years ago, the Program in Visual Arts at Princeton University invited me to develop a graphic design course, which didn't exist on campus. Trying to get the new class approved ran into friction at first, with the administration worried that graphic design was simply a trade, applicable to future employment perhaps but not up to the rigor of the rest of the undergraduate curriculum. In some ways, fair enough. Graphic design can be taught as simply a set of skills, emphasizing only mechanical and technical facility. But that's selling it short.

Instead, graphic design can be treated as a liberal art, by which I mean a subject to study, a body of knowledge that, when mastered, informs everything else you think about. Perhaps it's the most liberal of arts—

it has no real subject matter of its own, and graphic design is always working with outside content. It's a method applied to working with other subjects. In some ways, as a discipline, it is unmoored; free. I've heard it usefully, if circularly, described as "the discipline without the discipline of another discipline."

THE LIBERAL ARTS: A collection of seven subjects considered fundamental for the education of a free person in the Western collegiate tradition. These subjects are divided into two groups. Grammar, logic, and rhetoric comprise the human- ities. Arithmetic, geometry, music, and astronomy make up the sciences. Already named and formalized by the start of the Roman Empire, the Latin *liberalis* meant "free" and *ars*, "art or principled practice." The seven subjects are meant to foster broad thinking and encourage wide perspectives not only for addressing immediate problems, but also for identifying which problems are important. This tradition remains central to many contemporary colleges and universities.

A lot of the students who come to these classes won't go on to practice graphic design, but they do learn particular ways of thinking and seeing, some methods for approaching textual problems, visual problems, circulation and distribution problems, even computer interface problems. They can and do apply those skills to whatever else they study, and carry this sensitivity with them on graduation.

The graphic design curriculum developed at Princeton includes three basic courses. To describe these simply, T-y-p-o-g-r-a-p-h-y deals with letters and reading and writing; G-e-s-t-a-l-t has more to do with visual form and discrete graphic problems; and I-n-t-e-r-f-a-c-e is about computer interfaces, which I thought was an important enough subject now to justify its own class.

The courses evolved pretty organically and are presented in the order they were created. The first, T-y-p-o-g-r-a-p-h-y, sparked enough interest to warrant a second. That became G-e-s-t-a-l-t. Finally, I-n-t-e-r-f-a-c-e, the most recent, is an advanced class where students must have taken the other courses already.

The lectures that follow here (in pretty rapid fire, one after the other) have been refined and developed, adjusted and repurposed, over the semes- ters. Much of the material became either better, or at least more focused, by having to say it in front of a room full of sharp and skeptical minds. (It's immediately clear when it's not convincing.)

This certainly is not a carefully crafted collection of rules, guidelines, and methods intended to shore up graphic design as a relevant discipline. It is inevitably more of a digressive, discursive ramble, an occasionally high-speed pitch across any number of subjects and settings, though never possibly enough. Anyone else, by definition, would do this differently. It's limited, as much by my imagination and by my experience as by the practical constraints of a book. But in its form is also its argument. So let me be explicit: When you've finished *A *New* Program for Graphic Design*, rip it up, throw it away, and get busy assembling your own.

Now, let's get started.

T-Y-P-O-G-R-A-P-H-Y

I.

Typography has something of a split personality—it's both the technical act of writing words into the world by giving them form, and it's also a way of understanding the world through the forms of its writing. Designer Paul Elliman describes this two-way street concisely:

> Writing gives the impression of things. Conversely, things can give the impression of writing.

I'd suggest this reading and writing at the same time, or typography, is the root level skill of graphic design, and I'd like to talk about typography as something that joins reading and writing. Three modes of production will be presented in chronological order as a compressed reenactment of 500 years of typographic tradition, each one revolving around a particular technology: metal typesetting, phototypesetting, and digital typesetting.

The idea is to learn something about typography and therefore graphic design by practicing it, and along the way to understand how typographic techniques have changed over time in order to develop a nuanced facility in using the current digital tools.

We're going to start with Albrecht Dürer [↑]: painter, engraver, mathematician, goldsmith. He lived in Nuremberg and was a leading protagonist of the Northern Renaissance. I would also certainly call him a designer. This is *Melancholia I* [↓], a print from 1514.

Movable-type printing had been introduced in Germany only 75 years earlier. (It had already existed in China for 400 years at this point.) The production of typeset pages in multiple copies was still new, but as an engraver of metal printing plates Dürer was familiar with the process. This image has been reproduced many times and discussed, dissected, and deconstructed. What I like about it is something simple—it depicts a figure sitting still, kind of stymied.

It's been described as a spiritual self-portrait of the artist. The figure is surrounded by the tools of "the liberal arts" (grammar, logic, rhetoric, music, arithmetic, astronomy, geometry), but the artist is stuck—too much thinking, not enough doing. Melancholia indeed.

Allegorical objects are sprinkled throughout the image: an hourglass, scales, a large sphere and a so-called Dürer solid, a bell, a wax seal, a pen, and a compass. There's even a magic square, where all the rows and columns add up to the same number. In the bottom of the magic square are the numbers 15 and 14 [↙], which when read in sequence reveal the date of this work.

And on the lower far right is Dürer's signature [↗], a composite "A-D" monogram. This was engraved into the printing plates, so it's not a unique signature, but rather a printed mark with a specific graphic form.

Not long after *Melancholia I*, Dürer published *The Course in the Art of Measurement with Compass and Ruler*, [↑] in 1525. He addressed this four-book set to artists, artisans, architects, and "not only the painters, but also goldsmiths, sculptors, stonemasons, carpenters, and all those who have to rely on measurement." These were meant as practical guides, self-instruction manuals. The first book was on simple linear geometry. The second dealt with two-dimensional geometry. The fourth covered three-dimensional geometry. The third book is the strange one. Dürer called it "the little book," and it dealt with typography. *On the Just Formation of Letters* offers a geometric construction for the capital letters of the Roman alphabet. Other attempts had been made in Italy and Dürer was familiar with these efforts, but here he offered up his own prescriptions for constructing perfect, rational, geometric versions of each capital Roman letterform. Here is an "A" [↓].

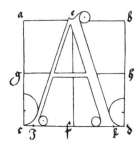 

At this time in Germany these Roman capital letters would have been strange. German writing didn't look like this. It used an alphabet of blackletter forms which were a reflection of the nibbed pens that wrote them. Writing was done by a person, not a machine, and a unique "hand" or signature was a proxy for the person.

Before movable-type printing, books were copied by scribes one by one. Dürer's books, however, were typeset and printed using individual metal letters [↗] which looked like handwriting, but were decidedly not handwritten. At the beginning of the 16th century, if you were used to seeing handwriting—as unique to the writer as her fingerprint—it must have been unsettling, eerie, and almost inconceivable to see writing mechanically reproduced. Each copy was identical, like a kind of perfectly multiplied individual. Seeing repeated mechanized writing must have had some of the uncanny character of what we experience with artificial intelligence and machine learning today. Here's another Dürer print [↙], *Death and the Landsknecht* from 1510, which captures something of that spirit.

The true *Effigies* of Iohn Guttemberg *Delineated from* the *Original Painting at* Mentz *in* Germanie.

The idea for movable-type printing arrived like "a ray of light" to German goldsmith Johannes Gutenberg [↗] in 1439 while he was busy trying to invent a magic mirror to capture the "holy light" from religious relics. His primary invention was an alloy for forging metal letters that was solid enough for printing and malleable enough so each could be melted and reformed as needed. Gutenberg's scheme leaked to Nuremberg, where Dürer's goldsmith godfather, Anton Koberger, set up a press and soon became the most widely distributed publisher of printed books in Germany. Printers decided what got printed, how it looked, where it went, and who was an author. Printing was power.

Printing has been called a "black art" ever since. The process used sticky, black ink and was messy. Its recipe for forging metal type from an alloy of lead, tin, and antimony seemed almost alchemical. And, perhaps most significantly, printing produced multiple, identical copies which persisted long after the individual author's death. Finally, printing was a closely guarded secret.

Or it was for a while anyway until British printer Joseph Moxon had a simple, if circular, idea: printing was a way to communicate ideas, so if other people knew how to print, there'd be more ideas circulating; and since he had a press and knew how to print, then he could print and circulate instructions for others teaching the art of printing. The result was a series of booklets called *Mechanick Exercises: Or, The Doctrine of Handy-Work Applied to the Art of Printing*, published in 1680. One in a larger series, the volume on printing self-reflexively used the process being described to talk about itself, and in the process, to spread the knowledge of how to print. In *Mechanick Exercises*, Moxon describes all the steps required to set up a printing press: how to make type, how to set up a type case, what to do with paper, and how to run a press. The booklets were sold by subscription and distributed. A letterpress shop today is (fundamentally) unchanged from what Moxon described in 1680.

* * *

OK. I'd like to summarize an article from *The New Yorker* by neuroscientist Oliver Sacks about Canadian detective novelist Howard Engel. One morning Engel picked up his newspaper and was surprised:

> The July 31st, 2001 *Globe and Mail* looked the way it always did.... The only difference was that I could no longer read what it said. The letters ... were the familiar twenty-six I'd grown up with only now when I brought them into focus, they looked like Cyrillic one moment and Korean the next.

Engel figured if this wasn't a practical joke (it wasn't), then he must have suffered a stroke (he had). He's admitted to the hospital, and soon discovered that although he cannot read, he can still write. Howard was incredulous: surely reading and writing went together. How could he lose one but not the other? A nurse suggested that he sign his name. He hesitated, but once started, the writing seemed to flow all by itself. The act of writing was surprisingly normal—effortless and automatic like walking or talking. The nurse had no difficulty reading what he'd written, but he could not read a single word. He continued to write every day in a "memory book" and soon developed the ability to read again through this act of writing. He also evolved a revealing coping mechanism:

> Occasionally with unusual words or proper names Howard might be unsure of their spelling. He could not see them in his mind's eye, imagine them any more than they could perceive them when they were printed before him. Lacking this internal imagery he had to employ other strategies for spelling, the simplest of these he found was to write a word in the air with his finger, letting a motor act take the place of a sensory one. Increasingly and often unconsciously, Howard started to move his hands as he read, tracing the outlines of words and sentences still unintelligible to his eyes. And most remarkable, his tongue too began to move as he read, tracing the shapes of letters on his teeth or on the roof of his mouth. This enabled him to read considerably faster, though it still might take a month or more to read a book he could have previously read in an evening. Thus by an extraordinary metamodal sensory motor alchemy Howard was replacing reading by a sort of writing. He was in effect reading with his tongue.

Reading and writing are intimately connected. There's probably a biological reason why we learn both at the same time.

* * *

This is the letter "T" [↘] drawn by my daughter when she was learning to read.

I was struck by her process and imagined that as she wrote the letter, she was also tracing the shape in her brain. American psychologist and pragmatist philosopher William James would say that she was actually inscribing these neurons; channels are opening up, widened by repeated use, and this habit is what allows the identification of these specific shapes as letters. Writing as reading as writing. We take it all largely for granted, but it can be very productive to consider exactly how strange and related these processes are.

Here's a diagram from William James' 1890 book, *The Principles of Psychology* [↘].

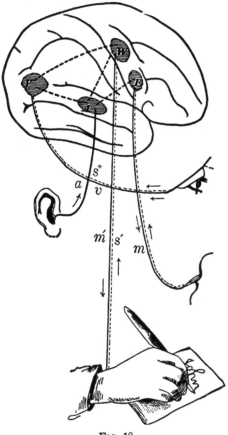

FIG. 18.

Something I was reading with my daughter at the time was *Charlotte's Web* by E. B. White. It's the story of an interspecies friendship between a special pig, Wilbur, and a cooperative spider, Charlotte. It's also a story about typography. Wilbur is a pig living on a farm. That's bad news for Wilbur. The morning he's due to be slaughtered, Charlotte decides that she needs to make the farmer realize that Wilbur is an exceptional animal. This is from the book:

> "If I write the word 'Terrific' with sticky thread, every bug that comes along will get stuck in it and spoil the effect. But now, let's see, the first letter is 'T.'" Charlotte climbed to a point at the top of the left-hand side of the web, swinging her spinnerets into position, she attached thread, and then dropped down. As she dropped, her spinning tubes went into action and she let out thread. At the bottom she attached the thread. This formed another attachment right next to the first. Then she carried the line down so that she had a double line instead of a single line. "It will show up better if I make the whole thing with double lines." She climbed back up, moved about an inch over to the left, touched her spinnerets the web, and then carried a line across the right, forming the top of the "T." She repeated this, making it double, her eight legs were very busy helping.

What's been described is the typographically robust first letter "T" in "TERRIFIC." Charlotte is living this typography by making it, and she offers a compelling account:

> "Now for the 'E.'" Charlotte got so interested in her work, she began to talk to herself as though to cheer herself on. If you'd been sitting quietly in the barn cellar that evening you would have heard something like this. "Now for the 'R.' Up we go, attached, descend, pay. Outline Whoa. Attach. good. Up you go. Repeat, attach, descend, pay out line. Whoa. Steady now, attach, climb, attach, overt to the right pay out line, attach, climb, attach, over to the right, pay, loop and around and around. Now into the left, attach, climb, repeat. OK. Easy. Keep those lines together. Now then, out and down for the leg of the 'R.' Pay out line, whoa, attach, ascend, repeat. Good." And so talking to herself the spider worked at her difficult task. When it was completed she felt hungry. She ate a small bug that she'd been saving and then she slept. Next morning Wilbur rose and stood beneath the web, he breathed the morning air into his lungs. Drops of dew catching the sun made the web stand out clearly. When Lurvy, the farmer's assistant, arrived with breakfast there was the handsome pig and over him woven neatly in block letters was the word "TERRIFIC." Another miracle. Wilbur was saved.

Postmasters

As it turns out, the day I wrote this was Benjamin Franklin's 300th birth-
day. Writer, typographer, printer, publisher, politician, inventor, statesman,
gentleman scientist, linguist, librarian, and the first Postmaster General of
the United States, Franklin was the consummate networker. Distributing
his ideas far and wide through a dizzying range of practices, he established a network of printing franchises by sending former apprentices
to set up shop in new towns and collecting dues. He traveled extensively
to London and to the courts of France, fostering alliances that helped
form a nation. He wrote incisive arguments and entertainments under a
constellation of pseudonyms including the Casuist, Silence Dogood,
Busy-Body, Poor Richard, and J. T. to suit the purpose at hand. He advo-
cated for a paper currency to facilitate the liberal distribution of goods
and services while he was also a printer and so stood to make money by
printing the paper currency which he lobbied for! He was often working
both sides of the equation and I think this compromised quality is what I
like about about this familiar engraving [↓]—his almost-smirk.

He published a weekly newspaper, an occasional magazine, and the
annual *Poor Richard's Almanack*. Along the way, Franklin pursued his
polymathic interests, inventing (a partial list): the medical catheter, the

armonica (a musical instrument), a phonetic alphabet, the circulating stove, swim fins, binoculars, and the lightning rod. He founded the first public lending library, a volunteer fire department, the American Philosophical Society, a university, and was the first Postmaster General of the United States. He was a committed generalist. This is his phonetic alphabet [↓], an attempt to make letters match one-to-one with the sounds of speech.

a b d e f g h i k l m n o p r s t u
[æ] [b] [d] [ɛ] [f] [g] [h] [i] [k] [l] [m] [n] [o] [p] [r] [s] [t] [u]

v z ɑ ɥ ɧ ŋ ɦ ɧ tɦ dɦ
[v] [z] [ɔ] [ʌ] [ð] [ŋ] [ʃ] [θ] [ʒ] [ʤ]

Benjamin Franklin was born in Boston in 1706, the youngest son of 17 children of Josiah Franklin, a candle maker and merchant. He studied briefly at Boston Latin School before being removed for more practical training. By age 12 he was apprenticed to his older brother James, a printer and publisher of the first independent colonial newspaper, the *New-England Courant*.

Initially, young Benjamin assisted with page composition, typesetting, leading, brushing, burnishing, and miscellaneous production tasks, receiving an intimate education in the mechanics of printing. James' busy shop was a nexus of pamphleteering. This was where you would come to engage in civic politics, to lobby for your point of view because this was also where your point of view would be printed and multiplied. Franklin realized this pretty quickly. The *Courant* provided the most widely distributed communication platform in Boston. As an increasingly competent writer himself, Franklin wished to add his voice to the public discourse circling around the print shop, but he knew his older brother wouldn't consent to print his writing, so he tried another tactic. Franklin assumed the alter ego Mrs. Silence Dogood, the dignified widow of a country parson. Writing under the pseudonym, he crafted a series of letters that were both entertaining and critical of Boston's Puritan establishment. Given his insider knowledge of the *New-England Courant* production schedule, Franklin carefully slipped the letters under the front door of the shop late at night.

The writing was funny and the content substantial. James Franklin published the first of 19 Silence Dogood letters on April 2nd, 1722.

Mrs. Dogood quickly gained a wide readership [↓].

Franklin began the initial letter with a sly acknowledgment of the power of the pen name, writing,

> And since it is observed that the Generality of People now a days are unwilling either to commend or dispraise what they read until they are in some measure informed by who or what the Author of it is, whether he be poor or rich, a Schollar or a Leather Apron man, &c. and give their Opinion of the Performance, according to the knowledge which they have of the Author's Circumstances, it may not be amiss to begin with a short Account of my past

Life and my present Condition, that the Reader may be at a Loss to judge
whether or not whether I know my Lubrication are worth his reading.

Franklin worked as a "printer's devil" in his brother's shop, typesetting
the newspaper. He also knew his brother had a weakness for humorous
writing. So he used this inside information—a combination of technical
skill and logistical knowledge—to set himself up as an author.

By the time the last Silence Dogood letter was printed in the *Courant*,
Franklin had unveiled himself as their author, much to James' displea-
sure. The younger brother now commanding too much attention, their
relationship fell apart. Benjamin left Boston without completing his
apprenticeship, went first to New York, and then on to Philadelphia,
where he arrived, in 1723, at the age of 17. He found printing work and
lodging with Samuel Keimer and soon established his own print shop.
By 1728 he'd befriended the governor, assimilated into polite society,
and established a modest living as one of three printers in Philadelphia.
As both a writer and printer Franklin enjoyed a privileged position from
which to distribute his ideas, which were rather distributed themselves.
He detailed the cyclical patterns of weather systems, and dispensed
sage advice, including the following in "Advice to A Young Tradesman
Written by an Old One" from 1748:

Remember that time is money.

Being intimately acquainted with the production process from writing
to reading to typesetting to page composition to printing, Franklin knew
that not only what was said or who said it was important, but to whom it
was said. Writing and printing would only take him so far. The real power
of print production, like any mass medium, lay in its distribution and the
primary network of the time was the postal system, which had grown
up around several colonial-era roads, including the Boston Post Road
(now U.S. 1). Unfortunately for Franklin's ambitions, he had a rival, Andrew
Bradford, who both published Philadelphia's only newspaper—the
American Weekly Mercury—and served as Postmaster of Philadelphia.

Bradford commanded access to news from afar while also directing the
network for distributing it. The result was a virtual monopoly on what was
news and who read it. Franklin contrived to reverse these circumstances.
He tried to set up his own newspaper, but he talked about it too much,
and when Samuel Keimer heard that Franklin was going to start a newspaper, he rushed to set up his own first: *The Universal Instructor in all*

Arts and Sciences: and Pennsylvania Gazette. Figuring Philadelphia was too small to accommodate three newspapers, Franklin resolved to eliminate one. Using his supple pen and exploiting the triangulated relationship between Keimer, Bradford, and himself—all rivals at this point—Franklin wrote a series of letters to the *American Weekly Mercury* under the pseudonym Busy-Body. The first letter began by suggesting the author's intent to enliven the paper's dull if respectable pages. He wrote,

> I design this to acquaint you that I who have long been one of your courteous readers have lately entertained some thoughts of setting up for an author myself, not out of the least vanity, I assure you, or of desire of showing my parts, but purely for the good of my country. I've often observed with concern that your *Mercury* is not always equally entertaining. The delay of ships expected in and want of fresh advices from Europe make it frequently very dull, and I find the freezing of our river has the same effect on news as on trade.

Once again, Franklin used humor, and Bradford printed his letters on the front page of the *Mercury*. They served to both boost the established paper and spurn the upstart *Gazette*, which at the time consisted largely of serialized encyclopedia entries. Keimer responded to Busy-Body's assaults in an increasingly shrill and desperate tone. The ensuing war of words left his newspaper in considerable debt. In 1729, Keimer was briefly imprisoned and fled to Barbados, selling his newspaper to Franklin as he was leaving town. The *Pennsylvania Gazette* then became Benjamin Franklin's newspaper and his mouthpiece, providing him a platform for his publishing, and over the years he developed a substantial reputation. By 1737 Franklin was appointed Postmaster of Philadelphia—he now commanded the central position that he'd angled for. He was a producer of the news with a proud tradesman's intimate knowledge of printing; he was a writer and knew the power of the pen; and he was Postmaster, directing and redesigning the networks of distribution. He was also busy doing a few other things at the time.

He gathered a group of his business associates under the name of the Leather Apron Club. This group of about 30 Philadelphians of relatively modest means was interested in reading. Books were expensive and they figured if they pooled their resources they could assemble a group of books that they could all share and read together. It made economic sense also, and the group's agreement formed the first lending library. The Library Company of Philadelphia circulated shared books, a new idea at that time. Franklin was also busy publishing *Poor Richard's Almanack,* the annual publication he authored under yet another pseudonym, Poor Richard. The popular guide [↓] was based around astrological tables for when to plant which crops as well as weather predictions. The weather charts are composed of dates and astronomical symbols with bits of text that run in between the two. These text fragments are what the *Almanack* is best known for. Franklin filled any extra space with pithy sayings and aphorisms ("A penny saved is a penny earned," "A friend in need is a friend indeed"), most of which he gets credit for and very few of which he actually wrote. These were common phrases but by reproducing them, they became his. Again, Franklin knew how to set type. He saw that he'd have extra room, and he decided to fill it, to great effect.

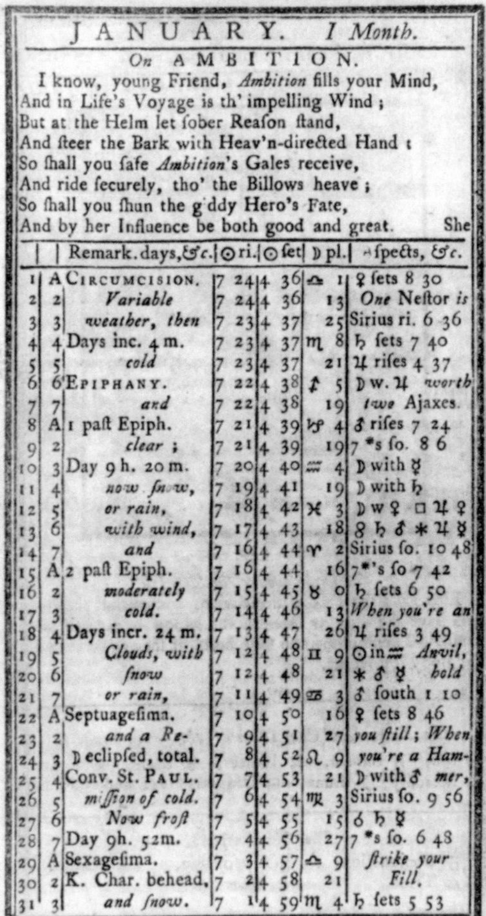

JANUARY. *I Month.*

On AMBITION.

I know, young Friend, *Ambition* fills your Mind,
And in Life's Voyage is th' impelling Wind;
But at the Helm let ſober Reaſon ſtand,
And ſteer the Bark with Heav'n-directed Hand:
So ſhall you ſafe *Ambition*'s Gales receive,
And ride ſecurely, tho' the Billows heave;
So ſhall you ſhun the giddy Hero's Fate,
And by her Influence be both good and great. She

		Remark. days, &c.	☉ ri.	☉ ſet	☽ pl.	Aſpects, &c.
1	A	CIRCUMCISION.	7 24	4 36	♎ 1	♀ ſets 8 30
2	2	*Variable*	7 24	4 36	13	*One* Neſtor *is*
3	3	*weather, then*	7 23	4 37	25	Sirius ri. 6 36
4	4	Days inc. 4 m.	7 23	4 37	♏ 8	♄ ſets 7 40
5	5	*cold*	7 23	4 37	21	♃ riſes 4 37
6	6	EPIPHANY.	7 22	4 38	♐ 5	☽ w. ♃ *worth*
7	7	*and*	7 22	4 38	19	*two* Ajaxes.
8	A	1 paſt Epiph.	7 21	4 39	♑ 4	♂ riſes 7 24
9	2	*clear;*	7 21	4 39	19	7 *s ſo. 8 6
10	3	Day 9 h. 20 m.	7 20	4 40	♒ 4	☽ with ☿
11	4	*now ſnow,*	7 19	4 41	19	☽ with ♄
12	5	*or rain,*	7 18	4 42	♓ 3	☽ w ♀ □ ♃ ♀
13	6	*with wind,*	7 17	4 43	18	☍ ♄ ♂ ✱ ♃ ☿
14	7	*and*	7 16	4 44	♈ 2	Sirius ſo. 10 48
15	A	2 paſt Epiph.	7 16	4 44	16	7 *'s ſo 7 42
16	2	*moderately*	7 15	4 45	♉ 0	♄ ſets 6 50
17	3	*cold.*	7 14	4 46	13	*When you're an*
18	4	Days incr. 24 m.	7 13	4 47	26	♃ riſes 3 49
19	5	*Clouds, with*	7 12	4 48	♊ 9	☉ in ♒ *Anvil,*
20	6	*ſnow*	7 12	4 48	21	✱ ♂ ☿ *hold*
21	7	*or rain,*	7 11	4 49	♋ 3	♂ ſouth 1 10
22	A	Septuageſima.	7 10	4 50	16	♀ ſets 8 46
23	2	*and a Re-*	7 9	4 51	27	*you ſtill; When*
24	3	☽ eclipſed, total.	7 8	4 52	♌ 9	*you're a Ham-*
25	4	Conv. St. PAUL.	7 7	4 53	21	☽ with ♂ *mer,*
26	5	*miſſion of cold.*	7 6	4 54	♍ 3	Sirius ſo. 9 56
27	6	*Now froſt*	7 5	4 55	15	☌ ♄ ☿
28	7	Day 9h. 52m.	7 4	4 56	27	7 *s ſo. 6 48
29	A	Sexageſima.	7 3	4 57	♎ 9	*ſtrike your*
30	2	K. Char. behead.	7 2	4 58	21	*Fill.*
31	3	*and ſnow.*	7 1	4 59	♏ 4	♄ ſets 5 53

Franklin's combination of on-the-ground knowledge and from-the-sky view served him extraordinarily well again and again. He soon graduated to Postmaster of Pennsylvania, and in 1753 he was appointed Joint Postmaster General for the Crown. As before, with his network of printers, constellation of pen names, and multiple business associations, Franklin succeeded in appointing friends and allies to many of the subordinate postmaster jobs throughout the colonies, ensuring himself a central privileged position at the hub of this increasingly critical distribution network. By 1760, Franklin had radically reorganized the postal service by establishing mile markers on roads and mapping new and shorter routes. Postal workers now carried the mail at night between Philadelphia and New York, cutting the delivery time in half, and developing post roads from Maine to Florida, New York to Canada. For the first time, mail between the colonies and England operated on a regular schedule with announced times, connecting the colonies to each other and to England, while at the same time beginning to articulate the still-unformed nation.

Along with all these improvements he was able to report an operating budget surplus to the Crown by 1760, the first time the Postal Service had made economic sense. By 1774, however, Franklin was relieved of his duties for actions sympathetic to the cause of the colonies. Shortly after, he was appointed Chairman of the Committee of Investigation to establish a postal system at the Continental Congress. On July 26, 1775, Franklin was appointed the first Postmaster General of the brand new United States of America.

In the words of the United States Postal Service today, "The current USPS descends in an unbroken line from the system Benjamin Franklin planned and placed into operation." As an independent branch of the executive branch of the United States government, the post office enjoys a de facto monopoly status on delivery of first class and third class letters, where long distance mail delivery rates are subsidized by delivery of very short distance mail, so you can send a letter from here to Kansas for the same price that you send it from here to Pasadena. Recently, increasing reliance on electronic communication has exerted substantial pressures on this distribution network, conceived and implemented 240 years ago by a Philadelphia printer.

The United States Postal Service remains, for the near future anyway, almost an anachronism—a network right at the edge of obsolescence, used every day, and still resembling a relic. Because of its curious status, it sheds some light on changing paradigms and patterns of information circulation. As a distribution network, the Postal Service is democratic, public, available, affordable, facilitates one-to-one asynchronous communication over a great distance, and is always on, efficient, economic, and—well—reliable [↓].

In their political self-help treatise from 2000, *Empire*, Michael Hardt and Antonio Negri examine a contemporary electronically networked condition where design, production, and distribution occur at one place and in real time. Suddenly writers can print their own text, designers can produce on the fly, and printers can distribute instantly what is needed, when it's needed, where it's needed. This generalist approach pries open a space of resistance for small actors in a massive system. Ideas can be designed, produced, multiplied, and distributed on demand.

Instrumental in the mass media of his day, in many ways Franklin was already there. Instead of concentrating resources and commanding an assembly line of content, design, production, and distribution, Franklin offered another approach—the networked tradesman. He was a highly skilled individual, committed to a trade, with an extended network of pre-occupations, assistants, pen names, jobs, friends, politicians, inventions, and hobbies. Look no further than the front page of the *Pennsylvania Gazette*, centered at the bottom margin, Franklin proudly added a byline where design, writing, production, and distribution collapse into one space and five words,

Printed by B. Franklin, Postmaster.

* * *

Beatrice Warde [↓] also used her frontline position in typography as a gateway to injecting her voice into a wider conversation through her writing.

Warde was born in New York City in 1900. Her father was an experimental musician from Germany who developed a chromatic alphabet. Her mother was May Lamberton Becker, a columnist at the *New York Herald Tribune* at the turn of the 20th century. Beatrice was often involved in her mother's work at the *Herald Tribune*, so she had an early appreciation for letters, for typography, for writing, and for editing.

After homeschooling until age twelve, Warde was sent to Horace Mann School, a progressive academy in New York City. She whizzed through her classes in Greek and Latin, everyday skills, and public service. She graduated in two years. From Horace Mann she went to Barnard College, which was a part of Columbia University. There she studied English, French, Latin, writing, and philosophy, among other subjects. Warde was something of a prodigy.

While at Columbia she met Frederic Warde. He was a printer and she was interested in typography. They married, and soon after graduating she went to work in the library of the American Type Founders Company in New Jersey [↘].

She was tasked with keeping track of all the type samples being made by the foundry, where they were producing not only the letters that others were using to print, but also books about typography. Soon Warde was the head librarian and the foundry's default publicist. She started to communicate widely about what the American Type Founders library held and why it mattered.

At the same time, her husband became the printer at Princeton University and was developing a significant reputation. He was encouraged by London-based typographer Stanley Morison to come to England and "expand his typographic palette." So, Beatrice quit her job at ATF, he quit Princeton, and they moved to London in 1924. Arriving in England, they shared an office with Stanley Morison and become inducted into a typographic circle. Frederic was given work designing two typography journals—*The Fleuron* and the *Monotype Recorder*.

THE "GARAMOND" TYPES
SIXTEENTH & SEVENTEENTH CENTURY SOURCES CONSIDERED

by

PAUL BEAUJON

It seems that so far this century has failed to establish one new type face to distinguish its books. There is a new style, but Caslon and the other stand-bys have been cast for three generations before ours. There are new advertising faces that represent faithfully our age and ideals: so faithfully that they are altogether unfit for book printing. It is among the revivals that we look for that chance of decent novelty that shall prevent us from seeing too much of the one thoroughly "English-speaking" type. Among the revivals three have unusual claims. Two of these, Baskerville and Fournier, are comparative

Meanwhile, Beatrice published an article in *The Fleuron* which questioned the sources of the Garamond types [↑]. She suggested that the types then attributed to Claude Garamond were actually designed 90 years later by Jean Jannon. Her article made a splash with its contentious ideas around a well-loved typeface. She also wrote it under a pen name fearing that she would not otherwise be taken seriously. She chose "Paul Beaujon," who she described as

> a man of long grey beard, four grandchildren, a great interest in antique furniture, and a rather vague address in Montparnasse.

Within a couple of years, Frederic started traveling to Europe more often and the two grew apart. They soon divorced and Beatrice stayed in London, where she continued to work with Morison, eventually becoming the editor of the *Monotype Recorder*. Like ATF, Monotype was also a type foundry and she was able to combine her technical knowledge with an ability to address the subject in an approachable manner to publicize good typography in England and to advocate for its use.

She began to communicate directly with printers to encourage them to update their approaches to typography. Ultimately, she was an ambassador for the use of considered typography [↓].

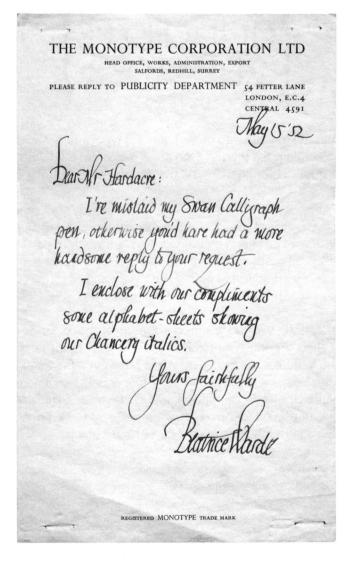

She became increasingly well known and struck up friendships with artists, typographers, and printers. British type designer Eric Gill was one, and together they created the successful publicity campaigns for two of Gill's typefaces, Gill Sans and Perpetua. In the meantime, Gill Sans has become almost a native typographic tongue in England—it appears everywhere from the London Underground to Penguin Books to

The *Monotype Recorder* masthead [↓].

THE
MONOTYPE
RECORDER

VOL. XXXII   WINTER 1933   NUMBER 4

Warde continued to write and publish around typography and printing in addition to editing the journal. One small pamphlet contains her most-often quoted thoughts around the dignity of typography. It reads,

> This is a printing office, crossroads of civilization, refuge of all the arts against the ravages of time, armory of fearless truth against whispering rumor, incessant trumpet of trade. From this place words may fly abroad not to perish on waves of sound, not to vary with the writer's hand but fixed in the having been verified by proof. Friend, you stand on sacred ground. This is a printing office.

On October 7, 1930, Warde delivered a speech at the St. Bride Institute in London called "Printing Should Be Invisible." Six days after she presented it, the lecture appeared in print in a Monotype publication. In 1937 it was republished as a stand-alone pamphlet and its name was expanded to "The Crystal Goblet, or Printing Should Be Invisible." This essay articulates one point of view for how typography should work. I'm not sure it's correct, but it's certainly persistent. Here's how it starts:

> Imagine you have before you a flagon of wine. You may choose your own favorite vintage for this imaginary demonstration, so that it may be a deep, shimmering crimson in color. You have two goblets before you. One is of solid gold, wrought in the most exquisite patterns. The other is of crystal-clear glass, thin as a bubble, and as transparent. Pour and drink; and according to your choice of goblet, I shall know whether or not you are a connoisseur of wine. For if you have no feelings about wine one way or the other, you will want the sensation of drinking the stuff out of a vessel that may have cost thousands of pounds; but if you're a member of that vanishing tribe, the amateurs of fine vintages, you will choose the crystal, because everything about it is calculated to reveal rather than hide the beautiful thing which it was meant to contain.

Assignment 1, Letterpress

Typeset and letterpress print "The Crystal Goblet, or Printing Should Be Invisible" (1955) by Beatrice Warde.

This assignment requires access to a letterpress print shop. Setting metal type and printing today is fundamentally unchanged from how it has been done for 500 years. Individual metal letters are combined in a composing stick upside-down and backwards, lines are assembled in a chase as a page, set on the press bed, sandwiched with wood-based paper, inked, reversed, and printed.

Week 1: Working in pairs, typeset one section of the edited text (approximately two paragraphs). Editing should be done to accommodate the number of students and divide the text evenly. All pairs work to the same line length, or measure, of 34 picas, and the same type size of 14 points with 2 points of leading between lines. Each pair will use a different font of type and these should be as mixed as possible given the resources of the shop.

Weeks 2, 3: Work through the stages of typesetting, proofs, and corrections iteratively with the assistance of the instructor to arrive at final prints of two paragraphs per group on one letter-sized page. The number of final prints depends on the number of students, one copy per student. Each pair will then design, typeset, and print one cover page using the same type size and font used to set the text. Its arrangement, editing, and graphic design are open. Print two copies of the cover page.

Week 4: Collate all printed pages to assemble complete sets of the group's collective work. Meet to read the text together, carefully considering Beatrice Warde's distinct ideas about how typography should work, filtered through the hands-on labor of the preceding weeks. Considering how slow and involved this typesetting process is should afford a much closer reading.

Farewell, Etaoin Shrdlu

Phototypesetting was always a transitional technology between metal and digital typesetting. It evolved through several stages, none of which ever really stuck. *Farewell, Etaoin Shrdlu*, a film directed by David Loeb Weiss, captures one moment in this transition by chronicling the last day of metal typesetting at the *New York Times* on July 2, 1978. The *Times* was moving away from Linotype machines and on to the next level of typographic automation, where a new system used a hybrid of computerized storage and photographic reproduction techniques to set all the words in the daily newspaper.

The film was shot entirely in the New York Times building in midtown Manhattan, where production was vertically integrated, in this case literally, as a series of stacked basements and sub-basements where typesetting, printing, bundling, and even distribution were handled. Daily production started from the editorial staff on the top floor and proceeded from one level down to the next, ending with delivery trucks pulling up to a loading dock and carting away bound papers for distribution.

```
LINOTYPE: An automated metal       stick, the operator uses a
typesetting machine invented in    90-character keyboard to assem-
1884 that sets individual char-    ble a string of matrices, or
acters as single lines of lead     letter molds. The line is then
type. Instead of setting let-      cast in hot lead as a solid
ters one-by-one in a composing     typographic printing slug.
```

```
MONOTYPE: An automated metal        of matrices that are cast
typesetting machine that casts      in hot lead. Unlike Linotype,
individual characters as            this machine produces indi-
discrete pieces of lead type.       vidual pieces of printing
The operator also uses a            type assembled together in
keyboard to assemble a string       a composed line.
```

It's useful to think about what these technical changes allowed for the distribution of news. What resulted from being able to set the paper so much more quickly? More editions per day? More money for reporting? Perhaps a rearrangement of physical space? Or more resources for long articles and also a broader range of quick-hit stories? Shifts in typographic technology inevitably provoke deep changes in what can be said, how it is printed, and what effects these printed words have in the world.

The film is approximately 30 minutes. It is narrated by veteran Linotype operator Carl Schlesinger.

I'd like to share a collection of excerpts now.

Schlesinger: We are fast approaching press time for the first edition of tomorrow morning's paper. This printer has just finished makeup of a page. In the next 56 minutes, all pages must be finished and recorded to meet the edition deadline of 9 p.m. But tonight's deadline is special. This *New York Times* mirror image in lead [↙] of tomorrow's dateline reads backwards as Sunday, July 2nd 1978. It marks the last day of an age-old method of printing in this composing room [↘]....

Makeup man: I find it very sad. Very sad. I've learned the new stuff, the new processes and all, but I've been a printer now for 26 years. I've been in this place for 20 years. Six years apprenticeship, twenty years journeyman. And these are words that aren't just tossed around, they've always meant something to us printers. I hate to see it. It's inevitable that we're going to go into computers. All the knowledge I've acquired over these 26 years is all locked up in a little box now called a computer. And I think probably most jobs are going to end up the same way.

Schlesinger: Do you think computers are a good idea in general?

Makeup man: Oh, there's no doubt about it. They are going to benefit everybody eventually, how long it will take, I don't know....

Schlesinger: Carefully, back on the stone where changes by the news department for the second, the late city edition. A galley of new type for a late breaking story is proofed up to be read for accuracy. Corrections are checked. Lines with arrows are replaced by corrected lines. And page one is ready to go again for the new deadline, 11 p.m. This time we follow it to the making of a stereotype mat. The mat is a damp sheet of flexible cardboard. A solid steel roller will press it against the hundreds of separate lines and picture cuts locked together in this page form.

Five minutes to the 11 o'clock deadline. The stereotyper taps down a spacing lead so that it won't print. The mat will soon be curved and dried into a half cylinder form. From it, curved, solid lead plates will be cast to fit on the rotary presses. The pressure of one ton per square inch is forced upon the cardboard. The raised lead type presses into the mat, forming a mold of recessed letters. The mat is now right reading and ready for casting.

Down into the stereocasting room, three stories below street level in the *Times* Building. Hot lead will now pour into the recessed impressions of type in this curved mat. Casting starts....

Worker 2: It's going to close up in the morning.

Schlesinger: How do you feel about it?

Worker 2: Another innovation. Another process we're moving into....

Schlesinger: This is goodbye [↖]. Generations of Linotype operators have often run their fingers down the first two rows of keys, releasing mats that read E-T-A-O-I-N, S-H-R-D-L-U. This fill out lines that start with keyboard errors. The last bad line is discarded at the end of the story. Motor off. A last touch of familiar brass mats. Lights out for good. It is the end of the age of hot type mechanical printing and the beginning of a new, the computerized cold type [↗]. The electronic. These seasoned printers, retrained, have made the transition from the old to the new....

The electronic images of letters that I have just set on this video display screen, I'll now send to the computer, where it is processed, stored, and brought back when required for corrections. Back to the computer. When needed, a touch of a key returns it to the editor. It is then changed to the desired column width, style, size of type, and hyphenation. Followed by further keyboarding of headlines and bylines. Then to one of five phototypesetters, each an electronic mirror. Inside, a web of components and wiring does the work of 140 Linotypes, generating a vast array of electronic type images on a concealed cathode ray tube [↙] [↘].

These images are contacted onto photosensitive paper at 1000 lines a minute, emerging from the dark room [↙]. The photo sensitized paper has now been transformed by a developing machine into photographic cold type, ready for full-page paste-up [↘]. This productivity leap, from 14 to 1000 lines a minute, is made possible several floors above by a battery of computers. These units contain magnetized memory disks and electronic digital systems which store and process all the data sent from below.

Switches and buttons, out of touch, bring us into an ever-advancing world of automation, computerization, and programmed electron flow. Humidity and temperature, monitored and controlled around the clock, are critical. These cabinets hold layered packs of yellow magnetic disks and others like this. The discs in operation spin at 140 miles an hour. More than a million words can be stored and sent back by each disc pack, and cold type on paper keeps on flowing. Photo technology has conquered hot metal. But typeset paper is cut, waxed on the back for adhesion, and pasted up on full page boards on these tables. From obituaries to sports, to the worlds of business, entertainment, real estate, classified and display advertising, and of course the news. Page after page will be run off on the high-speed rotary presses, as before, and folded into the finished page. But despite automation, computerization, and the continuing advances of electronics, the central factor is still the work of the human brain, the work of human eyes, and the work of human hands in creating that powerful element of communication, the printed word.

Raytracing with Moholy-Nagy

László Moholy-Nagy [↓] was a Hungarian artist, designer, writer, and teacher. He worked in Germany, England, and the United States.

This portrait from 1926 maybe reveals something of Moholy's disposition. He's wearing a workman's jumpsuit over a dress shirt and tie, looking like a hybrid worker-technocrat. He oriented himself more as a designer than an artist, although the distinction was fuzzy. He looks rather austere, but wasn't—his friends called him "Holy Mahogany."

Moholy was interested in photography. It was relatively new at the time and he recognized it as a contemporary way to make images. His photographic experiments often pushed at the edges of the medium. He exaggerated perspective and used unexpected vantage points to abstract the subjects he shot. He cut up prints and assembled collages. He gathered images into composites. And he made photograms.

Photograms are images made directly from, or, in fact, by, an object. The object is placed directly on photo-sensitive paper and then the paper is exposed to light. The result is a contact print, a kind of light tracing. American artist Man Ray developed the technique around the same time and he called them "rayographs."

 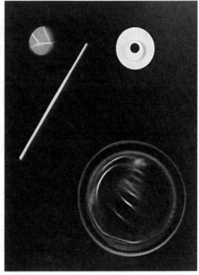

Here are two of Moholy's photograms [↖] [↗]. You might think of a photogram as seeing through an object to its essence. There's a one-to-one directness to the print, where the object is reproduced at the same scale as the image made of it. The process is immediate and the result has an equally urgent quality. It is not dissimilar from printing.

Moholy was also involved in design projects. He initiated Bauhausbücher (Bauhaus Books) in 1923, a provisional series of publications emanating from the German design school where he also taught. Moholy designed the format and covers for the series, and also designed the series' publicity materials. Moholy's cover for a prospectus booklet of 14 Bauhaus Books offered in 1928 is an exceptional typo-photographic image. It is

a composite photographic collage assembled from a multiplied image
of metal typesetting spelling out the series name. But metal type could
never look like this—by definition it must be "wrong-reading" so that when
it prints the words are legible. Moholy knew that if he made a photograph
and flipped the negative horizontally, he could create this uncannily "correct" type. He then doubled down, flipping the image vertically as well to
produce a compelling, if confusing, graphic arrangement [↓].

Around this same time, Moholy was also working on a motorized kinetic
sculpture. *Light Prop for an Electric Stage* [↙] is made from aluminum,
mirror, and glass pieces which are connected to a motor in the base and
rotate and move at various rates. When light is shined on the moving
sculpture, a constantly changing light pattern [↘] is produced.

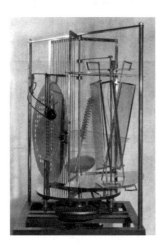 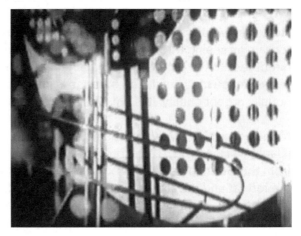

It is, like a photogram, a one-to-one translation of an object into light. In this case, the process is dynamic, as the machine is in motion. Moholy made still photographs from the sculpture as well as films. He worked with an engineer to design this apparatus, but the sculpture was clearly secondary to the images it produced.

* * *

Phototypesetting was invented by two French engineers, Louis Moyroud and Rene Higonnet, around 1946. On a visit to a local printer, the two had seen Linotype metal typesetting and thought surely the process could be improved with light and electricity.

They cobbled together a system from a typewriter keyboard and a strobe which used pulses of light through a negative film disk which had all the letters in a certain font. A key on the keyboard rotated the disk to show the correct letter. The light passed through the disk to photo-sensitive paper where the letter was inscribed. The result was a camera-ready letter. The process could be repeated quickly to produce a substantial phototypeset text. Simple.

This technology, even shortly after Moyroud and Higonnet introduced it, changed rapidly and never really settled into a longterm commercial application. There was already so much investment in automated type-setting equipment such as Linotype and Monotype machines, and entire production and printing processes would have to be completely scrapped to take advantage of the new system [↓].

Magnetic media could store what was typed into the phototypesetter. Electronic memory systems, including tape cassettes and floppy disks were bolted on. Soon enough computer front-ends appeared for photo-typesetting systems. There were lots of approaches.

Phototypeset text had a distinct graphic personality. Metal letters were cut individually at discrete sizes. So, perhaps 12 point, 14 point, and 16 point, but not 15.5 point, much less 15.1322 point. Phototypesetting, however, was fluid. Scaling was just a matter of pulling an enlarger back and forth. Type could be any size or it could be photographically distorted [↓]. Phototypesetting was also a bit coarser, and sans serif types became popular. Finally, the process made it less labor-intensive to design new fonts of type and many appeared during phototypeset-ting's heyday in and around the 1960s and 1970s.

Phototypesetting had another advantage. Metal letters can only sit so close to each other because they're set on a fixed body. Phototype, how-ever, is paper and so it can be cut to adjust the spaces between letters. Here's the mechanical typesetting of a stamp designed by Bradbury Thompson [↘]. Letters are carefully aligned and the spaces between are tightly condensed. This typography is a direct consequence of its setting.

I think that's enough for now.

Assignment 2, Photocopier

Re-typeset "The New Typography" (1923) by László Moholy-Nagy using a photocopier.

Phototypesetting was always a transitional typographic technology. Invented in 1946, the first machines used a typewriter keyboard to manipulate a glass disc with letters on its perimeter. When a key was pressed on the keyboard, the disc rotated to the corresponding position, light was focused through the disc onto photographic paper, exposing the letter. The result was camera-ready typography for making printing plates. Phototypesetting eliminated the heavy machinery required for automated metal typesetting and replaced lead with light.

Machines evolved rapidly, with media for storing previously typeset material and computerized front and back ends. Given the large investments in mechanical typesetting, phototypesetting was only ever a temporary solution. After less than 50 years, it was replaced by digital typesetting.

Weeks 1, 2, 3: Using only a black-and-white photocopier and digitally prepared printed type galleys, typeset the text as one or more letter-sized pages. When phototypesetting was most widely employed (c. 1960–90), type houses ran equipment to provide camera-ready galleys of a manuscript according to precise typographic instructions. Because type houses no longer exist, galleys will be provided as laser-printed sheets set in Monotype Grotesque according to six typographic specifications of measure and leading. Choose one as a starting point and use these galleys as raw material for reconfiguring this essay on the photocopier so that its meaning is amplified by its typesetting.

Week 2: Visit a library and review Moholy-Nagy's work, selecting one piece to present. Make a photocopy, bring it to class, and be prepared to speak about it. These images then become collective material for individual projects. Images can—and likely should—work together with typography in the completed project.

Week 4: Produce a final text as any number of one-sided photocopied letter-sized pages.

X-acto knives, glue sticks, and a large-format photocopier are required.

Originally published in *Staatliches Bauhaus in Weimar: 1919–23* (Munich, 1923), "The New Typography" is a short polemic by Lázló Moholy-Nagy which calls for the integration of typography and photography to produce a form of plastic writing as visual as it is literal. Moholy-Nagy was a constructivist, interested as much in how an image comes together as what the resulting image is. He was fascinated by photography, experimenting with photograms, abstraction, and camera-less image making. His graphic work pointed toward a future where writing would consist as much of images as letters, and where photos and text would be seamlessly synthesized into a new typography.

T as in Tree

Bruno Munari [↓] is a bit too well-known in the United States for children's books. He's less well-known for the breadth of his work. He was an artist, a designer, a writer, a teacher, an industrial designer, a TV host, and a curator working in Italy for most of the 20th century.

Around 1962 Munari wrote,

> Today it's become necessary to demolish the myth of the star artist who only produces masterpieces for a small group of ultra-intelligent people. It must be understood that as long as art stands aside from the problems of life it will only interest a very few people. Culture today is becoming a mass affair and the artist must step down from his pedestal and be prepared to make a sign for the butcher shop if he knows how to do it. The artist must cast off the last rags of romanticism and become active, well up in present day techniques, materials, and working methods. Without losing his innate aesthetic sense he must be able to respond with humility and competence to the demands his neighbors may make of him. The designer of today re-establishes the long lost contact between art and the public, between living people and art as a living thing.

This appeared in the Milan daily newspaper, *Il Giorno*, where Munari wrote a regular column on design. The excerpt I read was from an article titled "Design as Art." But he wasn't always so earnest. One was entirely visual and called "Trying to Find a Comfortable Position" [↓].

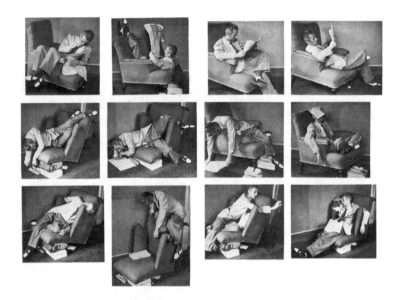

Munari's writing exists mostly in Italian, but "Design as Art" also became the title for a collection culled from his *Il Giorno* columns, translated into English, and published by Pelican in 1971 [↓].

In addition to writing in the newspaper about design, Munari was known for his workshops in museums, on live television, and in more traditional education venues like, you know, schools. He wrote and illustrated a series of books around these workshops. *Drawing a Tree* [↙] is one. It's a small book, modest even.

On the cover is a diagram of a tree broken into a series of branching operations. This diagram tells you immediately what you need to know to read the rest of the book. It then proceeds to do exactly as advertised in its title—tells you how to draw a tree. He offers a simple recipe at the start:

> The trunk divides into two limbs, each limb will continue to divide into two, getting smaller and smaller.

Periodically in the margins, the rule of growth is provided as a reminder:

> The branch that follows is always slenderer than the one before it.

Beyond this two-branching structure, there are trees which work in threes, fours, even fives. The method remains unchanged.

The idea is not, however, original—Munari appropriated it from "one of my very old countrymen, a certain Leonardo, born in a small village near Florence, Vinci (postal code 50059)." And he also included Leonardo's tree-branching drawing, which is more or less what Munari had redrawn for the cover. The material is nothing new, but he presents it with typical grace and wit.

Munari accounted for the basic underlying structure of a tree. Then he asked what happens in different specific situations? How about a tree that grows in a windy setting? Well, it looks like this [↓].

Or a tree that grows stretching for sunlight? [↙] The underlying branching structure is still visible.

Or a tree without leaves? A tree in winter? Another in spring. A tree struck by lightning? A perversely crooked one? [↓]

I like to imagine these trees as stand-ins for typefaces. Each tree family is also a type family with a collection of variations, all based on an underlying skeleton, and grouped around a clear structural concept.

In another essay from *Design as Art* called "Poems and Telegrams," Munari writes explicitly about typography [↓].

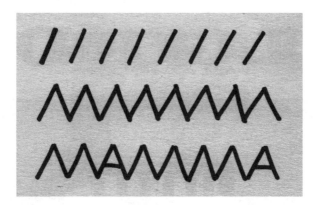

He's writing about how to speed up and slow down reading. You can render letters so that the message comes through quite quickly [↙].

And you can render the message so it arrives at a much slower pace [↙].

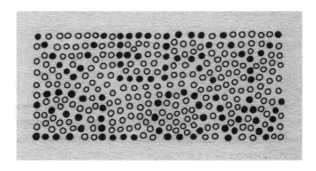

The essay is more of an instruction manual. Useful and lovely. Munari offers no real conclusions. I won't either.

This stands as a sketch for the future.

What follows is a work in progress, the product of one year at MIT's Center for Advanced Visual Studies tracing the legacy of graphic designer Muriel Cooper [↓]. It's organized as a guided tour of various sites on the campus of MIT, attempting to track 40 years of Cooper's work across different departments within the university.

Muriel Cooper always sought more responsive systems of design and production, emphasizing quicker feedback loops between thinking and making, often blurring the distinction between the two. OK, let's go ahead and get started.

1. An accidental archive at the Center for Advanced Visual Studies

We begin in a locked closet housing a collection of posters, documents, videotapes, and related printed matter which forms a de facto archive of the Center for Advanced Visual Studies. Embarking on a client-design relationship with the Center, I arrived in Cambridge to spend a few days going through the archive and examining its contents.

The Center for Advanced Visual studies was set up in 1967 by György Kepes as a fellowship program for artists. Initiated with considerable institutional and financial support, the Center produced artworks, exhibitions,

and public programs that were often accompanied by a poster or publication. These posters [↓] provide an immediate, condensed, and visually
legible accidental archive of its almost four-decade history.

While working my way through the contents of the closet, I was struck
immediately by the surface qualities of this extraordinary set of posters.
It was not simply the graphic design nor the typography that caught
me—rather it was their mode of production. The design of the posters
changed sporadically as new designers or administrators appeared,
but what remains the same is the way each self-consciously incorporates
its production method into the design.

For example, this poster [↑] revels in the extreme enlargement of a small sketch, photocopied large and produced on an offset press. The result is a tight and powerful synthesis of what is being said, how it is being said, and how what is being said is produced.

I assumed that many of these posters must have been designed by Muriel Cooper. I was already familiar with her work in broad outlines—I knew that she was the first Design and Media Director at MIT Press, where she designed *Bauhaus: Weimar, Berlin, Dessau, Chicago*, *Learning from Las Vegas*, *File Under Architecture*, and the MIT Press logo; she established the Visible Language Workshop and was founding faculty of the MIT Media lab; and that she died unexpectedly in 1994 just after presenting breakthrough work in new computer interface design.

As it turns out, I was mostly wrong about the posters' design—they were not designed by Cooper. Jacqueline Casey designed many of the early posters, and later ones were made by Otto Peine and others. However, many or most of these posters were printed at the Visible Language Workshop, a teaching and production facility in the Department of Architecture that Cooper cofounded with Ron MacNeil in 1975.

While poking around in the archive, I also learned that she was briefly a fellow at the Center for Advanced Visual studies. Her c.v. filed at the Center in 1974 lists "Interests and Goals":

> Concerned with use of mass production and its constraints and with extending experimental and educational experience into work relation- ships, reducing artificial human split. The significance of participatory and non-authoritarian communication forms in relation to specialization and professionalism. Structured/unstructured relationships in learning. Direct, responsive means of reproduction.

2. A sub-basement at the MIT Media Lab

We proceed by visiting the MIT Media Lab, where Muriel Cooper spent the last years of her working life, from 1985–1994, continuing the work of the Visible Language Workshop. I'm here to meet a graduate student who's procured a LaserDisc [↗] which includes some of the last work of the Workshop. With LaserDisc in hand, we spend the next hour or so trawling various sub-basements of the Media Lab building searching for an analog LaserDisc player capable of playing the 20-year-old media format. We enter more than one room containing stacks of outdated hardware, too difficult to repair, and rotting magnetic-tape formats whose chemical clocks are ticking. I am struck by the ways in which this recent past becomes so quickly inaccessible in a digital medium.

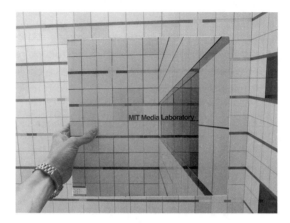

In stark contrast to the piles of posters that provide a visceral record of the Center for Advanced Visual Studies, these dead media provide nothing tangible. (As much of Muriel Cooper's most important work was in a digital medium, I become more convinced that accounting for her work is critical—now.)

We eventually score a working LaserDisc player and monitor. I press Play and after some fussing with an arcane remote control, the disc begins. Muriel Cooper appears on screen [↑] dressed in a graphic black-and-white polka-dot pattern offset by casually rumpled gray hair and reading glasses hung from a chain around her neck. Her voice is immediately enthusiastic and engaged.

Muriel Cooper: What we've begun to do is study ways in which rules can be modeled to the machine so that that machine will then begin to assume some of the responsibility for work which is repetitive or describable.

Man 1: We're working on a system which employs a rule base to assist in the process of graphic design and text layout. To do this we're using an expert system development tool called KESS and we've chosen the design of business cards to serve as a case study.

Computer voice: In what industry your profession? Financial, advertising, art, or science?

Man 1: Advertising.

Computer voice: What position do you hold?

Man 1: Management.

Computer voice: What is your company's financial scale?

Man 1: Medium.

Computer voice: What type of image would you like to project?

Man 1: Progressive.

Computer voice: Please wait while I get creative.

Man 1: Given the internal rules that we've put into the system it's decided that this particular layout is appropriate for me based on the answers I gave it. For example, the background of the card is gray rather than white and the text is left justified over on the right side of the card.

I go next down the hall to meet a longtime friend and colleague of Muriel Cooper's at the Media Lab and she begins by giving me some initial background on Cooper's working life.

On graduation from Massachusetts College of Art with a BFA in 1955, Muriel Cooper soon became involved in helping MIT develop a consistent visual language throughout its range of printed materials. MIT was heavily involved in government contracting after World War II and the volume of materials produced was significant. Beginning on a freelance basis, Cooper worked in the Office of Design Services from 1954 to 1957. In the first American university design program, Cooper helped develop a house style to make the technical language of much of the research produced at MIT legible for a wider audience. This work would be continued by her friend and former classmate [↓] Jacqueline Casey for 30 years.

Describing their time together as students at Massachusetts College of Art provides some clues to what comes after:

> I have always been frustrated and intrigued by technology. Jackie Casey and I both went to Mass College of Art in the late '40s. We were cashiers in the school store; we both eventually became bookkeepers—first Jackie and then me. We learned more in the store than we did in the school. In a way, I think of the school store as a model for the VLW. When the store would close in the afternoon, the students who worked there—about a dozen of us—had a studio to ourselves, our own little bin of paints and papers and materials.

In 1958, Muriel left MIT for Milan on a Fulbright scholarship to study exhibition design. Milan was then a lively center of contemporary ideas around product design, architecture, and new kinds of interactivity. Returning to Boston, she established Muriel Cooper Media Design in 1959. In her private practice Muriel returned again to work with MIT, a client sympathetic to her concerns and one that provided a natural platform for her work. She also began to work with MIT Press, designing book covers. By 1964, Cooper had also designed the MIT Press logo—a high-water mark in 20th-century graphic design.

3. A climate-controlled room at MIT Press

We continue on to the MIT Press archive, a small, clean climate-
controlled room at the offices of the Press. Beginning to the left of the
door and arranged on shelves circling the room clockwise sits every
book that MIT Press has published shelved in chronological order. The
overall effect is sublime—a committed reader might trace trajectories
of thought in biology, economic theory, computer science, or mathematics by circumnavigating the small room [↓].

Muriel Cooper became the first Design and Media Director of MIT Press
in 1967 and remained through 1974. Here she presided over the mass
production of a list of titles in architecture, economics, biology, computer
science, and sociology that formed a critical discourse around systems,
feedback loops, and control. (This was initiated a number of years prior
to her arrival with the MIT Press publication in 1948 of Norbert Weiner's
*Cybernetics: or the Control and Communication in the Animal and the
Machine*.) Her position provided her a platform to investigate the conditions under which these books were produced.

At the press, Muriel was able to directly engage the mechanics of mass
production and this quickly became her primary concern. Because of the
large number of titles published in one year and the relative slowness
of their graphic production, she was not able to be meaningfully involved

in the design of each book. Rather, she soon realized that efficient and responsive production systems had to be designed which would allow for the quantity of titles produced while maintaining a high level of design. She developed a rigorous classification and routing system for the design and production of books at MIT Press which identified and tracked projects along a streamlined process of design and production. By completely engaging the conditions of mass production and designing systems to account for them, she produced a consistently high standard of design across a very large number of titles produced at MIT Press during her tenure.

Often cited as the most successful design and production process of any university press, Cooper continually reevaluated how to make the conditions in which to produce good design work possible. Her work was then equally engaged in the production schedules, budgets, and conditions of production as it was in the typefaces, imagery, printing, and binding.

As a consequence, she was always searching for and implementing more responsive and iterative design and production processes at MIT Press. Frustrated by the delays that result from using specialized typesetting companies, she invented an alternate production method. In the late 1960s, the standard method of preparing a typewritten manuscript for publication involved sending out the raw text to a typesetting bureau. Given precise specifications, the typesetter would return camera-ready type galleys a week or more later to be pasted down into a layout back at the press. When there were corrections or copy edits, the type had to be returned to the typesetter to make adjustments and provide new galleys. Inevitably, the highly specialized labor of the typesetters was slow and therefore expensive. With the appearance of the IBM Selectric typewriter, Cooper imagined a more responsive design and production feedback loop.

For certain books in the late 1960s and early 1970s, MIT Press avoided typesetters entirely, bringing that role in-house by using the new electric typewriters with which Cooper was already experimenting. When a type galley required a correction, it was now only a matter of retyping the corrected section and the change could be made in a few hours rather than a few days. The corresponding savings in time, labor, and money changed the economics of publishing for books that could work in this alternate typesetting. A few of the better known examples of this work produced at the press in this manner include Herbert Muschamp's first book, *File Under Architecture* and Donis A. Dondis' *A Primer of Visual Literacy*.

These titles inevitably betray Muriel Cooper's deep investment in synthesizing design with an intimate knowledge of production. *File Under Architecture* was produced entirely with the IBM Selectric, where quick and immediate typeface changes were as simple as replacing the typographic ball. Margins were set in multiple typefaces as a running commentary. The book was printed on butcher's paper and bound in corrugated cardboard. The result [↙] looks like the process that made it and reveals a deep engagement with and symbiotic relation between the design and production of the book.

For *A Primer of Visual Literacy* [↗] all typesetting again was produced on an IBM at the MIT Press. However, this time the result is not immediately recognizable as typewriting. The book was set in a crude proportionally spaced version of Univers, the sans serif typeface designed by Adrian Frutiger (who also designed the standard Courier letters).

Perhaps the most visible mark that Cooper left at the MIT Press was the design of the publisher's mark in 1964. In an early sketch for the logo, a shelf of books is clearly legible, viewed from an idealized axonometric projection. A row of seven books sit neatly next to each other with (conveniently) the fourth pulled up and the fifth pulled down. The result is an abstracted form of the abbreviation "MITP" or MIT Press. Flattening the mark to form a series of positive bars of equal width results in a clear barcode—as the products of mass production sit together in an orderly row, dematerialized into the pure information of a machine-readable graphic. This important piece of graphic design already contained many of the concerns that Cooper would follow in the next 30 years probing the limits of mass production and exploring the impact of digital information [↙] [↘].

As a publisher's mark, the MIT Press logo is called a colophon. More generally, a colophon refers to the page of a book that details its production process—who typeset it, who printed it, when it was printed, what edition it is, library catalog references, etc. It is a convenient coincidence that Cooper's legacy at the Press is most clearly lodged in both of these colophons—on the spine in a highly formalized graphic and on the last page, where production details are tallied.

At MIT Press, there were yet some books with which Cooper would be personally and comprehensively involved as the designer. One prime example is *Bauhaus: Weimar, Dessau, Berlin, Chicago* by Hans Wingler published in 1968. Supported in part by an NEA grant and additional MIT Press funding, she would spend most of two years designing and producing the book. The "Bauhaus Bible," as it's widely known, contains the definitive collection of documents from the German art school through its multiple locations and bureaucratic arrangements. The book includes correspondence, descriptions of each workshop, budgets, and photographs documenting the spaces of the school. She described the subject matter of this book as a perfect fit, a coincidence of subject, designer, and situation. The book design was given enough time to happen in a comprehensive manner and the stunning result reflects it. Cooper described the fortunate synchrony of subject matter and design brief:

My design approach always emphasized process over product, and what better place to express this than in a tome on the Bauhaus, the seminal exploration of art and design in an industrial revolution.

Throughout the book design, production constraints were treated as design opportunities. Financial necessity dictated that the color plates be salvaged from a previous German publication. This determined the unusually large format of the book [↓].

On completing the book, Cooper made a film of its pages being flipped through to create a stop-frame animation. The book's contents shift around the page, defining the grid that structures its design. The Bauhaus book film was the after-image of her design process. It projected out from the hard physical form of the book to suggest a near-future when publishing would be as fluid as film, feedback immediate, and users and makers would be all but indistinguishable. This constant interrogation of the near-future as a tangible present, as a practical lens for producing in the present, powered a lot of her best work.

When she finished the book in 1968, she was left with the ethical residue of the Bauhaus and a clearer idea about teaching, production, practice, and the mutually dependent relationships between them. At the MIT Press, she had begun a small research unit where the experiments in IBM Selectric typesetting, computerized layout, and other modes of book production were explored by designers, students, and computer programmers. This proto-workshop that mixed practice, research, and production convinced her that a more ambitious workshop within MIT might be possible.

A few years later, she began to explore the possibility of establishing a similar situation in the Department of Architecture at MIT. In the margins of a draft memo to the department head proposing a visual communications center, a set of handwritten notes flushes out some of her goals for the nascent workshop:

1. Media design and print design@conceptual stage
2. Educational pretext—WORKSHOP
3. Publishing
4. Interdisciplinary? INSTITUTE/RESOURCES

4. A flat file labeled "Muriel" at the MIT Museum

The next stop is the MIT Museum archives. It's just one floor down from the Center for Advanced Visual studies in Building N51 and adjacent to one of Muriel Cooper's former workspaces. Inside, just to the left of the door is a double-stacked flat file [↓] filled primarily with teaching documents simply labeled in Sharpie and masking tape: "Muriel."

By 1974, Cooper had partnered with designer, artist, and technician Ron MacNeil to teach a new graphic design class at MIT Department of Architecture called Messages and Means. MacNeil came to MIT in 1966 as Minor White's technical assistant while setting up the Creative Photography program. He completed his degree in 1971 and apprenticed himself to the Architecture Machine Group established by Nicholas Negroponte to learn computer programming. In the next three years, he acquired and installed two single-color, sheet-fed offset printing presses in an empty room with double-wide doors next to the photographic darkroom in Building 5. With overlapping interests and mutual friends, Cooper and MacNeil met, and the idea to teach a design class together centering around these printing presses emerged.

Cooper had already been teaching at Massachusetts College of Art, but was frustrated by how undergraduate design students froze when beginning an assignment. As soon as they were put into a situation of hands-on production such as using a photocopier or making monoprints, they became considerably more free.

She was convinced that a workshop environment [↑], where teaching happens in a feedback loop with hands-on production and design would work well. MacNeil's significant technical background in printing, photography, and, increasingly, computer programming, plus access to an offset printing press made this possible. Cooper described the goals of the Messages and Means course as:

> Design and communications for print that integrated the reproduction tools as part of the thinking process and reduced the gap between process and product.

Messages and Means students learned in a workshop environment how the printing press works by using it. Opening up access to this instrument, students were able to explore an intimate and immediate relationship to the means of production for their design work. The inevitable result was a merging of roles and blurring of specializations. In the workshop, students became editors, platemakers, printers, typesetters, and designers all at one time, in overlapping and iterative configurations.

> They used the offset printing press as an artist's tool: they collaborated on platemaking and they altered the application of inks—they rotated the paper to make printing an interactive medium.

Messages and Means introduced production-led assignments literally centered around the printing press that occupied most of the classroom. Students were asked not only to design their assignments, but also to work with the printer, darkroom, and typesetting machines to produce their project. For example, students made "one-night prints," skipping the traditional stages of design, paste-up, and pre-press by working with presstype and photostatic cameras or exposing the printing plate directly. Students were independent, motivated, and empowered to realize their projects as they wished [↓]. As a result, the course was consistently over-enrolled.

Messages and Means students constantly circulated between the offset printing press room and the adjacent photographic pre-press room. The trip required leaving one room, walking 20 feet down the hall, and entering the other, only to arrive on the other side of a shared wall, five feet away. During the Independent Activities Period of January 1976, a group of (perhaps) over-zealous students took matters into their own hands to remodel this unfortunate architecture, demolishing the wall that stood between the two rooms. Literally tearing an unsanctioned hole through the middle of the MIT Department of Architecture and Planning, the students fused these two spaces. The combined workshop mixed the inks, noise, paper, and mess of offset printing with photographic enlargers, typesetting machines, chemicals, and increasingly elaborate electronics and computer systems. In this space, the activities of designing, teaching, and producing became increasingly indistinct. This was the Visible Language Workshop [↓].

The Visible Language Workshop, a unique interdisciplinary graphics laboratory, was founded to explore verbal and visual communication as information and as art on both personal and public levels. The synthesis of concept and production processes is informed by tradition and technology.

Muriel Cooper was appointed Associate Professor in the Department of Architecture in 1981 and after seven years in Building 5, the VLW was offered a bigger space Building N51 with the Center for Advanced Visual Studies and Nicholas Negroponte's Architecture Machine Group. Five years later, the VLW moved again, this time into Building E15, the MIT Media Lab.

With the establishment of the Media Lab in 1985, Negroponte convinced Cooper to join as one of several principle research areas within the ambitious venture. Negroponte was insistent that the VLW take on a different name as the Media Lab was to be a place for developing new media, its new forms, new consequences, and new possibilities. Cooper refused—the concerns of the VLW were precisely the same within the Media Lab as before, even as the context for their work was shifting from the printed page to the computer screen.

The catalyst for much of the early computer work at the VLW was a large-format printer designed by Ron MacNeil. Called The Airbrush Plotter, this printer could produce billboard-sized prints from digital files. He secured $50,000 from the Outdoor Advertising Association of America in 1979 to build a prototype and it was working within six months. After four years, the total project funding was around $500,000. (Computers were much more expensive then—MacNeil recalled spending $125,000 on a Perkin Elmer 32-bit super mini-computer!) This funding buoyed other pursuits as the VLW moved into a much larger facility in Building N51.

By 1979, MacNeil and a group of graduate students were also hard at work on a software platform for image and text manipulation. Called SYS, this proto-Photoshop program developed the functionality of large and expensive "paintbox" programs in a more immediate manner. Workshop members began to use it, and the proximity of the users of SYS and the makers of SYS allowed for short cycles of refinement and development with powerful feedback loops [↓].

Cobbled together with help from students in Electrical Engineering and the Architecture Machine Group, SYS was a hard disk and a computer memory management scheme that yielded an image workspace of 8000 × 2000 pixels. SYS also included a single line scanner built to capture the high-resolution images needed for billboard-sized output on The Airbrush Plotter.

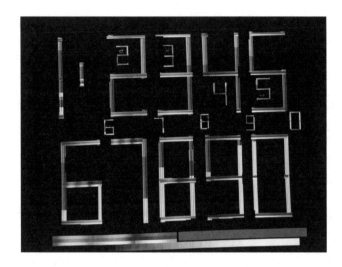

Building on previous digital printing experiments, the VLW experimented with a remote digital printing technique called Slowscan [↑]. It was more like an oscilloscope than a photograph—where the CRT printer instantly exposed an image on the screen to the paper, Slowscan slowly built up the image by scanning one line at time onto the photographic paper from an electronic file. The communication between machine and printer was necessarily slow, requiring a minimum of bandwidth. As a result, transmission of these images would be possible over long distances between a sending computer and a receiving printer. Slowscan prints were transmitted from Boston to São Paolo, Vancouver, Tokyo, and elsewhere. What began as an experiment in digital printing had become a transmission medium, pointing the way forward to a very near future when digital images were no longer made for printing, but instead created for distribution through electronic networks.

5. A Small Design Firm on Massachusetts Avenue

In a storefront on Massachusetts Avenue in Cambridge, halfway between the campuses of MIT and Harvard, is the office of Small Design, Inc. I have come to speak to David Small after hearing that he had a "closet full of Muriel Cooper things." As a student, researcher, and collaborator in the Visible Language Workshop, Small contributed extensively to many of its most important projects. He began as an undergraduate in 1985, joining the VLW in 1987 and completing his PhD in 1999.

By 1985, the Visible Language Workshop had become one unit in the ambitious new Media Lab. Negroponte described the goals of the Media Lab in *Design Quarterly* 142 (guest edited by Muriel Cooper) in 1989:

> The Media Laboratory is a pioneering interdisciplinary center that is a response to the information revolution, much as the Bauhaus was a response to the industrial revolution.

Where there was once only a single Perkin-Elmer computer, there were now several Hewlett Packard workstations and even access to a super-computer, the massively parallel Connection Machine 2 (CM-2). Still, Cooper insisted that the new space remain a workshop.

On moving into Building E15, they found a space which was considerably more corporate than their previous home in N51. E15, also known as The Jerome Wiesner building, was designed by I. M. Pei and looks much more like a suburban low-rise office (wrapped in a multi-colored ribbon by artist Kenneth Noland) than it does a university laboratory. Inside, relatively low drop-ceilngs, wall-to-wall carpeting, systems office furni-ture, and an atrium lobby amplify the effect. Cooper insisted that the VLW would be organized differently. David Small remembers how the physical space mirrored Cooper's teaching style:

> She was a different kind of teacher: very reluctant to tell you what to do. Once you've started with the assumption that there's no right or wrong way of doing anything, what becomes more important is getting students to think on their own. Muriel set up the right kind of environment for that: the space encourages interaction.

The Visible Language Workshop at the Media Lab skipped the low-lighting and cubicles of the other units, opting instead for an open-plan to house the ad hoc collection of computers, typesetters, and printers that had accumulated in the previous 11 years. Large power drops even hung from the conference room ceiling waiting to power the offset print-ing presses which never arrived. Already the concerns of the workshop were moving increasingly into software and communication patterns that remained completely within the architecture of the computer. Ron MacNeil recalls,

> In time, images stay on the screen. And now they travel through networks. I think what Muriel finally discovered was the act of communication design in the process of radical change away from creating single artifacts to

creating design processes that need to have a life of their own over these networks.

Previous projects had begun to make it clear that electronic communications moving fluidly through networks of readers, writers, users, and makers offered the communication space that Cooper had been trying to find for years. The workshop continued to explore the relationships between what gets said and how it gets said, but in their new home, the VLW left behind the printed page for the fluid space of the computer screen.

> You're not just talking about how the information appears on the screen, you're talking about how it's designed into the architecture of the machine, and of the language. You have different capabilities, different constraints and variables than you have in any other medium, and nobody even knows what they are yet.

The Visible Language Workshop began to design interfaces which offered routes, pathways, or even self-guided tours through this soft architecture.

> In the early days of MIT Press, designers had worked hard at understanding how to direct the viewer's eyes in two dimensions: X and Y. The computer posed the challenge—and offered the opportunity—for the designer to create more complex pathways through multi-dimensional information. This had been the distant gleam in the eye of past workshops and it was realized here.

6. The Muriel Cooper Archive at Massachusetts College of Art

Finally, we arrive where I probably should have begun—The Muriel Cooper Archive at Massachusetts College of Art. The small room at her alma mater is stacked with banker's boxes too high to reach and a set of flat file drawers with oversized materials. Among the totally mixed contents of each box—file notes, sketches, slides, production schedules, mechanical artwork—I'm reminded that Cooper's greatest asset may have been her refusal to specialize.

She recognized that the discrete roles which industrialized production of the assembly line had delegated to its workers were beginning to dissolve. Desktop publishing softwares had opened up professional-level graphic production to a much wider audience, and designers were left with room to expand their practice.

Among these boxes [↑], I found an original copy of the piece that Cooper and the Visible Language Workshop produced in 1980 for *PLAN*, the journal of the MIT Department of Architecture. When asked to submit an article about the Visible Language Workshop, she responded instead with a 12-page visual essay produced together with students in the workshop, using the tools of the workshop. The first page of the article reproduces a letter that she wrote to the editor describing the VLW's submission. She lists four numbered points that describe the goals of the visual article that follows, but she may as well be describing the 40 years of her own practice:

July 15, 1980 ...

1. It would make use of the tools, processes and technologies of graphic arts media as directly as possible and the tools would be integrated with concept and product. Many of these are in the workshop....

2. The author would be the maker contrary to the specialization mode which makes the author of the content the author, the author of the form the designer, and the author of the craft the typographer/printer.

3. Visual and verbal representation of ideas would be synthesized rather than separate.

4. Time would remain as fluid and immediate as possible, leaving room for feedback and change.

She concludes the letter [↓] cordially, signing off with a promise:

This stands as a sketch for the future.

July 15, 1980   Jeffrey L. Cruikshank
                     Editor, Plan
                     School of Architecture & Planning
                     MIT, 7-233

Visible Language Workshop
Room 5-411
Massachusetts Institute of
Technology
Cambridge, Massachusetts
02139

Dear Jeff:

When you asked me to prepare an article for Plan, I set myself the
task of producing a "graphic" article which would represent the
ideas and concerns of the Visible Language Workshop by virtue of
its form as well as its content.

In a computer electronic age we see print communication as a model
of changing user/maker relationships and the workshop as a place
in which the content, quality and technology of communication inform
each other in education, professional and research programs.

The article, "Words, Images, Tools and Ideas" would try to fulfill
the following criteria:

1. It would make use of the tools, processes and technologies of
graphic arts media as directly as possible and the tools would be
integrated with concept and product. Many of these are in the
workshop. In this case, they include a heavy use of all forms of
photography and our computer graphics system for both images and
typography.

2. The author would be the maker contrary to the specialization
mode which makes the author of the content the author, the author
of the form the designer, and the author of the craft the typo-
grapher/printer.

3. Visual and verbal representation of the ideas would be
synthesized rather than separate.

4. Time would remain as fluid and immediate as possible, leaving
room for feedback and change.

Much of the material was developed together with Professor Ron MacNeil
and the VLW staff. It has been a fascinating opportunity which has
elucidated many of the complexities of authorship into print. There
is still no magic way – but we propose to keep working at it.

This stands as a sketch for the future.

Best Wishes,

Professor Muriel Cooper
Director

Assignment 3, Computer

Typeset "On Typography" (1967) by Herbert Bayer twice, using contemporary digital typesetting software.

Digital typesetting arrived with the introduction of the Apple Macintosh personal computer in 1984. It replaced phototypesetting which existed for the previous 50 years, while metal typesetting had persisted for almost 500 years. Setting even a short text in metal type is very slow. Phototypesetting is considerably faster. Now with digital typesetting, it has accelerated exponentially and, as a result, information circulates much faster. On the internet and over networks, information arrives so quickly that typographic templates must be designed for updated material to automatically flow into. This assignment requires working faster, typesetting one text in two different ways over two weeks.

Week 1: Begin with "On Typography" by Herbert Bayer. Closely read the text in order to typeset it as any number of letter-sized pages in a way that reflects and amplifies its arguments.

Week 2: Read "The Principles of The New Typography" by Jan Tschichold. Do not re-typeset Tschichold's text but rather apply Tschichold's arguments to a second typesetting of Bayer's "On Typography" text. Understand and decide how the two Swiss typographers' approaches are similar and how they are different. These insights should inform the two typesettings. The two will likely be related but must also be distinct. The final product is two versions of the same text produced as any number of one-sided laser-printed letter-sized pages.

Herbert Bayer was an Austrian graphic designer and typographer who immigrated to the United States in 1946. He was a committed modernist: designing books, type, exhibitions, buildings, and interiors, as well as writing and speaking around his convictions. "On Typography" is equally direct. Bayer argues for an uncompromising approach which dictates the structure of text on a page, its arrangement in columns, subheads, and sections. He provides a collection of typographic prescriptions, including sans serif type, the reduction of weights to a minimal set, and the diminished contrast of type with its background to produce a universal typography that's smooth, refined, consistent, and eminently modern.

In "The Principles of The New Typography," Jan Tschichold also argues for a modern conception of typography, although his differs from Bayer's in some ways. Unlike Bayer, Tschichold advocates a pronounced use of contrast, type size, and rules to emphasize the hierarchies of information in a text. Where Bayer's approach to typography could be applied universally to any number of texts, Tschichold suggests a more contextual response. He argues that the setting of a given text should be determined directly from a close analysis of its form and should use all of the tools of modern graphic typography to clearly convey its internal structure.

Mathematical Typography

Computer scientist and Stanford professor emeritus Donald Knuth's early digital typesetting experiments had a big impact on how we set type today. He also suggested a typographic path not taken. This was how he began his Josiah Willard Gibbs lecture at the American Mathematical Society on July 4, 1978:

> I will be speaking today about work-in-progress instead of completed research. This was not my original intention when I chose the subject of this lecture, but the fact is I couldn't get my computer programs working in time. Fortunately, it is just as well that I don't have a finished product to describe to you today because research in mathematics is generally much more interesting while you're doing it then after it's all done.

It's a prestigious lecture awarded annually for individual contributions to applied mathematics and when Knuth faced the room of mathematicians assembled in Providence, Rhode Island, he proceeded to talk not about math, but instead about typography. He began by showing slides, one after the other, pages from *Bulletin of the American Mathematical Society* illustrating how its composition and typography has changed over the last 100 years. For example, he showed this page from 1922 [↓] and pointed to its sharp modern serif type.

THE JOSIAH WILLARD GIBBS LECTURESHIP

The Council of the Society has sanctioned the establishment of an honorary lectureship to be known as the Josiah Willard Gibbs Lectureship. The lectures are to be of a popular nature on topics in mathematics or its applications, and are to be given by invitation under the auspices of the Society. They will be held annually or at such intervals as the Council may direct. It is expected that the first lecture will be delivered in New York City during the winter of 1923–24, and a committee has been authorized to inaugurate the lectures by choosing the first speaker and making the necessary arrangements.

R. G. D. RICHARDSON,
Secretary.

These were typographic fine points likely lost on his audience. But he had a reason, or an agenda anyway. He was showing these because he was upset by how the journal looked now. The *Bulletin* had switched to photo-typesetting and Knuth found the result so (typographically) poor, that he refused to publish his work in it.

Knuth [↗] talked not just about the typography in the journals, but also about a project he was working on to improve the prospects for digital typesetting. The "work-in-progress" he alluded to at the start of the talk, a new digital typesetting system, continued for the next 10 years. He discussed a few specific problems along the way in precisely describing subtle curves in the shapes of letters [↙] [↘].

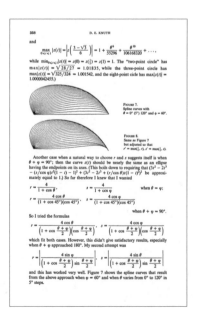

For example, the curve in the middle of an S is tricky. Knuth shared his attempts with quadratic, cubic, even quartic curves to mathematically describe that shape. So, it wasn't that he didn't show any math or talk about math, but he did so only in service of the typography.

Knuth was already well-known for this set of books called *The Art of Computer Programming* [↓]. It's from 1970.

These have been called "the Bible of computer programming." I've had a student describe them to me concisely as: "A set of hypothetical books about computer programming—where if there's such a thing as a computer, and if there is a computer language, and if you are going to write a computer program in that computer language, then this is how you would do it." The books traffic in first principles. They are language agnostic and provide basic ideas—almost *ethical* ideas—about how you should construct a computer program. These books have been critically important for the development of computer science. They have also been fundamental to the softwares, hardwares, and computer languages that have been programmed since.

The books address fundamental algorithms and basic software design patterns for computer programs. They are principled, logical, and thorough. They are also funny. For example, on the first page of volume 1 is a flow chart for reading the books [↓].

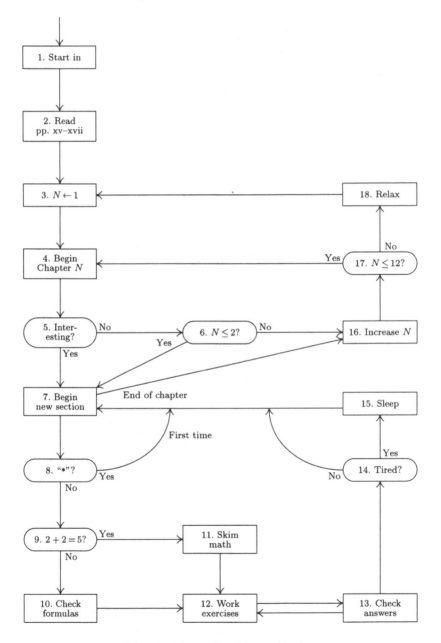

Flow chart for reading this set of books.

The first edition of *The Art of Computer Programming* was typeset in metal by a Monotype specialist in England who dealt with mathematic texts and the special typographic demands of formulas, equations, and proofs. This first edition proved commercially successful and a second edition was planned for 1977. In the meantime, Knuth's publisher had moved on from metal to phototypesetting and the whole production process changed. Usefully, Knuth kept a diary around that time which he later published with annotations. Here is his entry from the day he received page proofs for the second edition [↓]:

My diary of 1977 says nothing more about typographic matters until March 30; on that day, however, the die was cast.

30 Mar: Galley proofs for vol. 2 finally arrive, they look awful ... I decide I have to solve the problem myself. ↱typographically Seder supper at church, is a bright spot in dull week.

I had to devote the month of April to finishing the other projects I had started. But by the beginning of May I had decided to create a program called 'TEX', and I was gearing up to embark on a new adventure.

Knuth was horrified by the quality of the new phototype. He also realized that setting a page of type is a discrete problem. Divide the page into a fine grid of squares—each box is either black or white, ink or no ink, 1 or 0. Here's a zoomed view of type on a laserprinted page [↙].

With its binary logic, this was a perfect problem for a computer program. Knuth had a six-month sabbatical coming up and figured he could program his way out of this typesetting dilemma. And if he managed to do it, he would have an perfectly reproducible version of his typeset book which could be updated for future editions at the end of the six months.

It didn't quite turn out that way. Knuth worked on the project for the next 10 years before handing it off to to an open group of collaborators. The resulting digital typesetting software is called TeX. People loved it.

They still do, and it remains extensively used throughout academic publishing particularly mathematics, science, and computer science. TeX is powerful, simple enough, and a pleasure to work with [↙].

It uses a markup language, something like HTML. Heads, subheads, and body are identified by the author. Bolds and italics indicated. Semantic relationships in the text are tagged and then TeX does the dirty work of formatting the text. TeX was designed for mathematics, so formulas can be entered directly and TeX will typeset it correctly. Setting mathematics manually is tedious, so this was a boon. TeX also appeared considerably before other digital typesetting softwares and many of its fundamental algorithms, particularly for setting justified type, were incorporated into a series of consumer softwares from Aldus FrameMaker to PageMaker to Quark Xpress to Adobe InDesign.

METAFONT

Knuth designed a second program to work with TeX as a helper app. Metafont [↗] is a tool for designing and generating typefaces by describing them mathematically. TeX puts type on a page and Metafont draws that type. Metafont also runs on its own. It's built on the underlying metaphor of handwriting and uses a skeleton form for each letter specified as a set of related parametric equations. Here's [↙] a skeleton for the letter "A".

Metafont then traces this using a software "pen" to make the letter. A thin round pen looks like this [↑]. A chisel pen [↑] at 30° like this. And a heavy round pen with points shifted right looks like this [↗].

Knuth created Metafont software in order to mathematically describe a typeface he called Computer Modern and then to use it as the default type for TeX. He soon realized that letterform design was considerably more difficult than he expected. He recruited experts including Hermann Zapf to help him along. Here's a clipping of Knuth and Zapf studying a Computer Modern ligature on February 14, 1980 [↓].

An early version of the numbers from Computer Modern drawn by Metafont demonstrate a few issues [↓]. The "8" is particularly wonky.

0123456789

Because Metafont defines a set of related points as a program, and because it uses that program to generate letters on the fly, then Metafont can also *change how it behaves as it runs.* So it's possible to, for example, typeset the digits of Pi so that they get smaller and smaller receding into infinity [↘].

3.1415926535889 79:2..·—

Letters could be adjusted to coarser or finer resolutions. And randomness could even be injected into the letterforms directly. I'm not sure why you'd want your mathematics to look like like a tiki bar in Orange County, but maybe it's good to know that it's possible [↓].

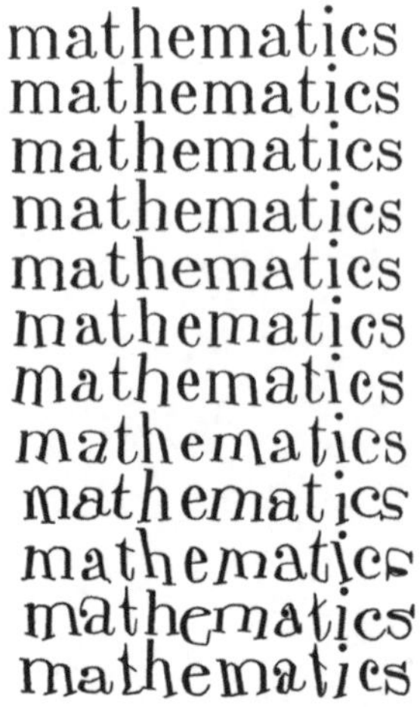

mathematics
mathematics
mathematics
mathematics
mathematics
mathematics
mathematics
mathematics
mathematics
mathematics
mathematics
mathematics

The same Metafont (one collection of letter skeletons) could be rendered as serif or sans serif or even a hybrid halfway between the two while retaining its internal geometry which could also be skewed [↙].

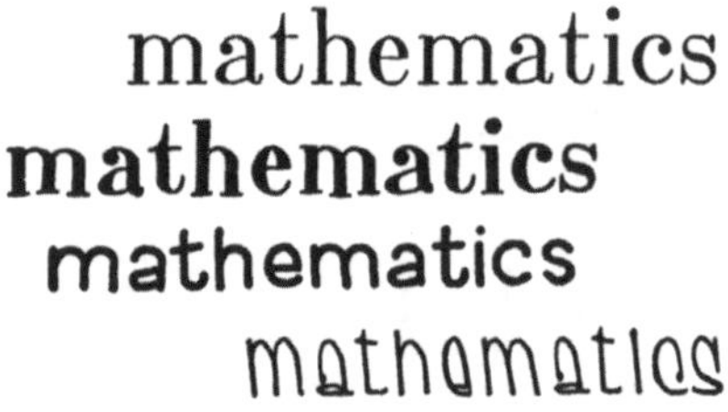

mathematics
mathematics
mathematics
mathematics

Metafont, however, never really took off. Its mathematical learning curve proved a bit steep for type designers. And mathematicians were not necessarily so interested in designing typefaces. It remains an alternate typographic future.

Returning to Knuth's journal [↓] from June 30, we find him still struggling with that capital letter "S." He writes,

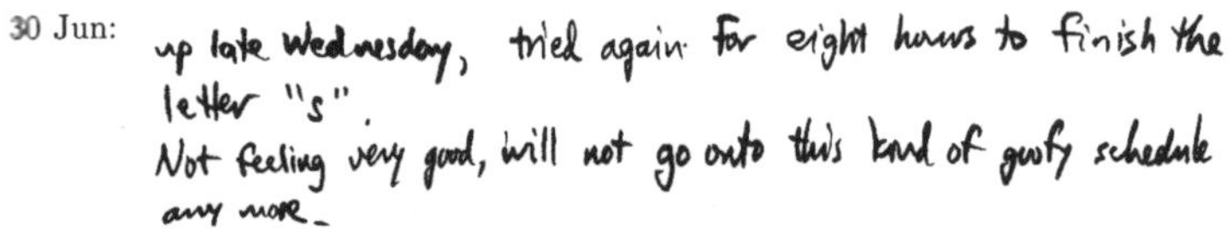

30 Jun: up late Wednesday, tried again for eight hours to finish the letter "s".
Not feeling very good, will not go onto this kind of goofy schedule any more.

The next day he continues,

1 Jul: Hurray, success on ess after 4 hrs. calculations (4:30 am today). Made me feel better.

And finally,

2 Jul: Cleaned up font program, added punctuation, put it away. Slept and slept

When Knuth finally resolved Metafont, TeX, and Computer Modern to his initial satisfaction, he published an article. It was (of course) typeset in TeX with Computer Modern using Metafont. The title of the article was simply "The Letter S" [↓] and it begins with a large capital "S." This is also exactly what he is talking about as the article recounts the technical subtleties of mathematically constructing that letter. It's funny and warm. It's technically precise. It's typeset with software he designed, set in type he designed, and rendered by a program he designed, all the while describing the process of designing all of this. The reader comes along for the ride. I like it a lot.

114
The Letter S

Donald E. Knuth

SEVERAL YEARS AGO when I began to look at the problem of designing suitable alphabets for use with modern printing equipment, I found that 25 of the letters were comparatively easy to deal with. The other letter was 'S'. For three days and nights I had a terrible time trying to understand how a proper 'S' could really be defined. The solution I finally came up with turned out to involve some interesting mathematics, and I believe that students of calculus and analytic geometry may enjoy looking into the question as I did. The purpose of this paper is to explain what I now consider to be the 'right' mathematics underlying printed S's, and also to give an example of the META-FONT language I have recently been developing. (A complete description of METAFONT, which is a computer system and language intended to aid in the design

.1., con quello tondo quale ha lo suo puncto de mezo fora del quadro, longe da la inferiore linea del quadro puncto mezo. Poi largo lo circino puncti .2., ponendo una puncta dove finisti la inferiore parte del .S. qual fu facta a drita linea, cioè longe da la linea del spacio da parte drita puncti .2., e altri

* * *

There are several qualities of Metafont that I find beautiful and I was interested in trying to use it; to pick up where Knuth left off and to figure out what could be done with it now. The best way to learn about something is often to take it apart and put it back together for yourself. In this case it was already broken. Originally released in 1979, the software was radically out of date. Metafont didn't usefully run on contemporary computers because it was geared towards pixel-based bitmapped output devices and, in the intervening 30 years, computer displays and printers had moved on. Documentation for the original Metafont software also falls in a funny gray zone. The project was finished before the internet became widely accessible. Printed documentation was difficult to track down at first and so I fumbled around. All told, it took about six months to rehabilitate the software—to assemble the various pieces, update these for contemporary operating systems, to assemble a program to trace the shapes of the bitmap characters, and then to produce a once-again working Metafont.

The investigation was a joint effort together with Stuart Bertolotti-Bailey, a designer I've collaborated with for the last 10-plus years under the shared name Dexter Sinister. Here's a double self-portrait as triangles called *A Primer of Visual Literacy* [↙] [↘].

When the software was finally working, we named our new, updated version of Metafont with an absurdly long new name: Meta-the-difference-between-the-two-Font. The name was borrowed from a profile of David Foster Wallace in *The New Yorker*. Foster Wallace describes his writing as:

> Not realistic, and it is not metafiction; if it's anything, it's meta-the-difference-between-the-two.

This phrase has just enough sense that it keeps you thinking. I love things like that. Anyway, Meta-the-difference-between-the-two-Font is not really different than Metafont, except it runs on a contemporary computer. It took a lot of work to get to that point, many wrong turns, and no shortage of digressions. I suppose this is also the point. And as often happens when designing a speculative project, Meta-the-difference-between-the-two-Font found a number of other situations to be used over the following few years. Each time, we developed the font a bit. I want to run through a whole collection of these now as I think that the way this project keeps moving is also what it is about. Here's how it looks [↓].

Meta-the-difference-between-the-two-Font

The motivation to do this work with Metafont came through an invitation for Dexter Sinister to participate in an exhibition at the Queens Museum of Art called *The Curse of Bigness*. We suggested making this typeface as our contribution and to use it for the graphic design of the exhibition. Here's the new typeface in vinyl for the title [↓].

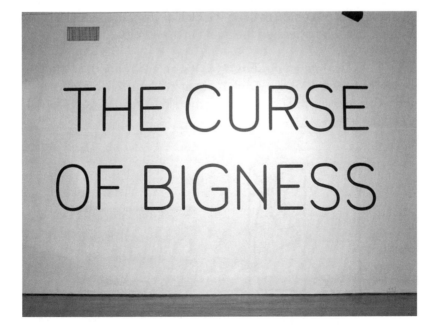

It was also used for an interim signage system installed throughout the museum while it was undergoing a renovation project of its own.

We also used it to typeset the catalog [↓].

Next, it was set as blocks of text on a wall at The University of Illinois Chicago's Gallery 400 for a Dexter Sinister exhibition called *The Plastic Arts*. Timed to coincide with the opening of that show in Chicago and the show at the Queens Museum, we asked the curator from the Queens Museum to lead a virtual tour of the exhibition in Chicago. We built a scale model for her to use and connected an iPhone whose camera was broadcasting to a projector, making it look like you were actually in the gallery for those who attended the event in my studio.

We next wrote "A Note on the Type." [↓] It's an essay about Meta-the-difference-between-the-two-Font, typeset in Meta-the-difference-between-the-two-Font. That was published in *Dot Dot Dot*, a journal we edited at the time.

About six months later, Stuart and I started a new publication together with artist and writer Angie Keefer called *Bulletins of the Serving Library*. "A Note on the Type" was updated and reproduced in the first issue alongside a new companion text we wrote called "A Note on the Time." It was about how computers agree on the time over a network.

We were next invited to do an artist's project for an art fair in Turin, Italy. Our response was to have all of the vinyl signs set in our Meta-the-difference typeface. That was done, and the typeface appeared through-out the art fair. But then we added a second part to the project which was a small exhibition of vinyl type on the wall which functioned as a kind of walk-in caption for the signs. We called it "A Note on the Signs." Here's what the type looked like installed at the art fair [↓]:

In Turin, Kadist Art Foundation asked about buying the typeface for their collection. We suggested a more complicated arrangement. We would use the invitation as an excuse to develop an aspect of this project we'd been interested in—to make the typeface explicitly *change over time.*

We upped the ante a bit more by insisting that Kadist take Meta-the-difference-between-the-two-Font as their logo for the next 10 years. This typeface—and therefore their logo—would then change very slowly over that time.

We would continue to make the software run for 10 years, which is not a given with any piece of code, while they would vow to not change their logo for 10 years, staying the course as this font evolved. Here it is at four points over the first five years [↓].

KADIST

KADIST

KADIST

KADIST

In thinking about how to put this thing in motion, we imagined several changeable parameters. With Meta-the-difference-between-the-two-Font, you can change the weight, you can change the slant backwards and forwards, and you can change what's called the superness, or the roundness of the "O," which then affects all of the other letters. We imagined the slant, superness, and weight as the three axes of a cube with a little ball that does a random walk through that possibility space, between any of those parameters. As the dot moves, then the "pen" parameter also changes moving from a nib to a point, etc. slowly over time. We developed this as a computer program as well, and the result looks like this [↓]—we called it Meta-the-difference-between-the-two-Font-4-D, lopping on a couple more letters to what was already a too-long name.

Meta-the-difference-between-the-two-Font-4-D

Meta-the-difference-between-the-two-Font-4-D

Meta-the-difference-between-the-two-Font-4-D

Meta-the-difference-between-the-two-Font-4-D

The following year, Meta-the-difference-between-the-two-Font-4D ended up at the Museum of Modern Art in New York, where it was further developed as part of an exhibition called *Ecstatic Alphabets: Heaps of Language.* This was a show organized around artists using typography where Dexter Sinister was offered a central commission. Together with Angie Keefer as The Serving Library we produced an issue of our journal as an exhibition catalogue comprised of 13 commissioned texts around typography, all typeset in our "house font" [↙].

Stuart and I also wrote an expanded article [↗] called "Letter & Spirit" about the development of the 4D-version of our typeface which was included in the catalog. The new text merged "A Note on the Type" with "A Note on the Time" to address how letters can and do change over time. We also produced a video which was included in the MoMA exhibition that acted as a trailer for the exhibition catalog. This was an 18-minute animation which presented excerpts from the 13 articles using the Meta-the-difference-between-the-two-Font-4-D animated typeface.

The font was next included as part of the annual Graphic Design Festival in Chaumont, France. We were invited by Swiss graphic designer, programmer, and artist Jürg Lehni to use a machine he had adjusted to etch computer files onto 35mm film. His machine could record a series of pages from a PDF file onto film to produce a typographic animation.

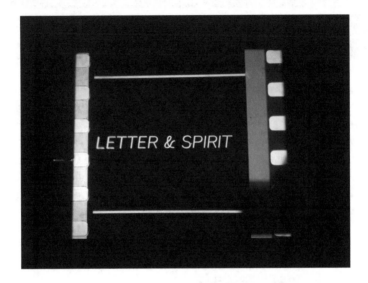

Given the opportunity to use the relatively old technology of film for a typographic animation, we decided to use Meta-the-difference-between-the-two-Font-4-D to speak both for and about itself in a short animated essay called "Letter & Spirit." This film [↑] condensed the original text (of the same name) into 18 minutes where Meta-the-difference-between-the-two-Font-4-D is used to tell the story of its creation, placing the font within the broader context of attempts to rationalize and reform the letters of the Roman alphabet over the last 500 years. "Letter & Spirit" wrestles with what is the point of rehabilitating an existing (and anachronistic) software, and exactly how the new version is any different from the original version.

Through writing about it, through making it, and through editing both what we made and what we wrote, we arrived at an unlikely conclusion which still seems plausible: although Meta-the-difference-between-the-two-Font-4-D is fundamentally indistinguishable from the original Metafont, the new work remains essentially different because embedded within the new version is also the complicated, digressive, discursive, even meandering backstory of how it came to be what it is. I remain convinced, both as a teacher and also a practicing designer, that, when so much is so readily available, these stories are how we make coherent sense of what we do.

Further Reading

Bayer, Herbert. "On Typography (1967)," in *Herbert Bayer*. Cambridge, MA and London: MIT Press, 1984.

Bringhurst, Robert. *The Elements of Typographic Style*. Point Roberts, WA: Hartley & Marks, 1996.

Dondis, Donis A. *A Primer of Visual Literacy*. Cambridge, MA: MIT Press, 1973.

Elliman, Paul. "My Typographies," *Eye* magazine 27, Spring 1998.

"Farewell, Etaoin Shrdlu," New York Times video, 29:17, October 13, 2016, https://www.nytimes.com/video/insider/100000004687429/farewell-etaoin-shrdlu.html

Franklin, Benjamin. *Benjamin Franklin's Apology for a Printer: Reprinted From the Pennsylvania Gazette of June 3-10, 1731*. Philadelphia: Philosophical Hall; printed by A. Pomerantz & Co., 1953.

Froshaug, Anthony, and Robin Kinross. *Anthony Froshaug*. London: Hyphen, 2000.

Gerstner, Karl. *Designing Programmes: Four Essays and an Introduction*. London: Tiranti, 1964.

James, William. "Habit," in *The Principles of Psychology*. New York: Dover Publications, 1950.

Kinross, Robin. *Modern Typography: An Essay In Critical History*. London: Hyphen Press, 1992.

Knuth, Donald. *Digital Typography*. Stanford, CA: Center for the Study of Language and Information Publications, 1999.

Lupton, Ellen, and J. Abbott Miller. "Laws of the Letter," in *Design Writing Research*. New York: Kiosk, 1996.

Moholy-Nagy, László. "The New Typography," in *Staatliches Bauhaus, Weimar, 1919-23*. Weimar-München: Bauhausverlag, 1923.

Moxon, Joseph, Theodore Low De Vinne, and Elmer Adler. *Moxon's Mechanick Exercises; Or The Doctrine of Handy-Works Applied to the Art of Printing: A Literal Reprint In Two Volumes of the First Edition Published In the Year 1683*. New York: The Typothetæ of the City of New York, 1896.

Panofsky, Erwin. *Albrecht Dürer*. 2nd ed., rev. Princeton, N.J.: Princeton University Press, 1945.

Reinfurt, David, and Robert Wiesenberger. *Muriel Cooper*. Cambridge, MA: MIT Press, 2017.

Sacks, Oliver. "A Man of Letters," *The New Yorker*, June 26, 2010.

Tanchis, Aldo, and Bruno Munari. *Bruno Munari: Design As Art*. Cambridge, MA: MIT Press, 1987.

Tschichold, Jan. *The New Typography: A Handbook for Modern Designers*. Berkeley: University of California Press, 1995.

Warde, Beatrice. *The Crystal Goblet: Sixteen Essays On Typography*. London: Sylvan Press, 1955.

White, E. B., and Garth Williams. *Charlotte's Web*. New York: Harper, 1952.

http://www.t-y-p-o-g-r-a-p-h-y.org

So, it starts like this:

I stand at the window and see a house, trees, sky. Theoretically I might say there were 327 brightnesses and nuances of color. Do I have 327? No, I have sky, house, and trees. It's impossible to achieve 327 as such. And yet even though such droll calculation were possible and implied—say for the House, 120, the trees, 90, the sky, 117—I should at least have this arrangement and division of the total not say 127 and 100 or 150 and 177. The concrete division which I see is not determined by some arbitrary mode of organization lying solely within my own pleasure. Instead I see the arrangement and division which is given there before me [↙].

And what a remarkable process it is when some other mode of apprehension does succeed. I gaze for a long time from my window, adopt after some effort the most unreal attitude possible, and I discover that part of the window sash and part of a bare branch together compose an "N." Or look at a picture.

Two faces cheek-to-cheek [↑]. I see one with its, if you will, 57 brightnesses and the other 49 brightnesses. I did not see an arrangement of 66 plus 40 nor 6 plus 100. There have been theories which would require I see 106. In reality I see two faces. Or I hear a melody, 17 tones with its accompaniment, 32 tones. I hear the melody and accompaniment not simply 49 and certainly not 20 plus 20 plus 9. And the same is true even in cases where there is no stimulus continuum. I hear the melody.

Or one sees a series of discontinuous dots [↑] upon a homogenous ground, not as the sum of dots, but as figures. Even though there may have been a greater latitude of possible arrangements the dots usually combine in some spontaneous, natural articulation and any other arrangement even if it can be achieved is artificial and difficult to maintain. When we are presented with a number of stimuli we do not as a rule experience a number of individual things—this one and that. Instead larger holes separated from and related to one another are given an experience. Their arrangement and division are concrete and definite.

This is an excerpt from what's known as the "Dot Essay" from 1923, written by Czech psychologist Max Wertheimer, and more accurately known as "Investigations in Gestalt Principles," or "Laws of Organization in Perceptual Forms." It's a strange text that shifts between letters and dots. The dots assemble and reassemble into constellations that read more like sentences—initiating, picking up, or expanding on an idea. Although the text is didactic and intended to be instructive, it has a restive quality. Since it is performing the subject matter that it's also attempting to explain, it's hard to make it stay still. And through its shifting nature, the text articulates the fundamental Gestalt qualities, which describe how distinct groupings of the same dots can be seen to be related to one another.

GESTALT QUALITIES: There are eight principles in "Laws of Organization in Perceptual Forms" that describe how discrete elements produce coherent groups: 1. Proximity — differences in relative distance; 2. Similarity — based on visual form; 3. Combination of Proximity and Similarity — distance and form simultaneously form units; 4. Common Fate — expected behavior based on perceived lines of force; 5. Prägnanz — salience, coherence, and resolved shapes form units; 6. Einstellung or Set — repeated, rhythmic exposure produces groups; 7. Good Continuation or Closure — completion of elements into coherent, stable groups; 8. Past Experience — prior exposure conditions the recognition of current groupings.

I. A row of dots is presented upon a homogeneous ground. The alternate intervals are 3 mm. and 12 mm.

 (i)

Normally this row will be seen as *ab/cd*, not as *a/bc/de*. As a matter of fact it is for most people impossible to see the whole series simultaneously in the latter grouping.

We are interested here in what is actually *seen*. The following will make this clear. One sees a row of groups obliquely tilted from lower left to upper right *(ab/cd/ef)*. The arrangement *a/bc/de* is extremely difficult to achieve. Even when it can be seen, such an arrangement is far less certain than the other and is quite likely to be upset by eye-movements or variations of attention.

 (ii)

This is even more clear in (iii).

 (iii)

I.e. :—

	c	f	i	l	o	
---	b	e	h	k	n	etc.
	a	d	g	j	m	

Quite obviously the arrangement *abc/def/ghi* is greatly superior to *ceg/fhj/ikm*.

Another, still clearer example of spontaneous arrangement is that given in (iv). The natural grouping is, of course, *a/bcd/efghi*, etc.

 (iv)

Resembling (i) but still more compelling is the row of three-dot groupings given in (v). One sees *abc/def*, and not some other (theoretically possible) arrangement.

(v)

While on vacation in 1910, Wertheimer was traveling on a train toward Frankfurt when he saw an arrangement of flashing lights at a railroad crossing circling around a rectangular frame, much like the lights on a theater marquee. Instead of a series of individual light bulbs illuminating in sequence, what Wertheimer "saw" was one light moving around the frame. He was struck by the phenomenon and thought to himself,

"Why does that light appear to be moving? I know this is just a bunch
of individual bulbs lighting up in order, but why do I perceive only one dot,
one light, moving around in this pattern?"

Wertheimer [↗], who was interested in such things as how we intuit
movement from a series of discrete perceptions, was immediately cap-
tivated by the question. He abandoned his vacation, got off the train
in Frankfurt, found a hotel room, and went straight to a toy store to buy
a zoetrope [↘].

A zoetrope is a device which holds a sequence of individual pictures
spaced around the interior of a rotating cylinder. There is a viewing
slot on the outside so that only one of these frames is visible at any
moment. When the cylinder is spun, the drawing appears to move.
Wertheimer altered his zoetrope by replacing the images with a set
of austere drawings, each with two vertical lines in the frame. He wanted
the lines to appear as though they were moving in tandem when the
zoetrope was in motion, and he wanted to know the precise moment

when this illusion breaks down. Exactly how far apart can you draw the lines between any two consecutive frames before the movement stops? How few steps could you get away with so that it still feels like the two lines are moving together?

This simple setup was the genesis of many of his later Gestalt experiments. Wertheimer steadily probed the limits of perception, asking what is the difference to the viewer between "real" movement and "apparent" movement; between an object in the world as it physically moves and the perception of an object moving produced through sequential exposure to a set of discrete frames. Is "apparent" movement just an illusion or is it real? If so, how could the reality of apparent movement be proved?

Wertheimer realized that what matters is the whole experience, including the in-between moments, and that movement is produced by the dynamic interrelations between any of its individual, constituent parts. As he moved the lines closer or further apart on the zoetrope, Wertheimer saw that there is a critical moment at which many people begin to see the lines moving. This inflection point varied slightly with each person, but it was within a consistent range. Then he got a bit more professional about it. Wertheimer stopped into the Psychological Institute in Frankfurt, introduced himself as a colleague, and asked for space to work on some ideas while he was on vacation. (It turns out Wertheimer remained at the Psychological Institute quite a lot longer than he expected. Two other psychologists working there at the time, Wolfgang Köhler and Kurt Koffka, also became deeply involved in the work and the three continued to work together closely for the next five years.)

Experiments were upgraded to a tachistoscope, a more precise zoetrope, which allowed the accurate projection of individual images to the subject with very fine-tuned timing. The trio repeated and refined their experiments, examining the limits of when movement appears or not. What they discovered—the big breakthrough—was that *apparent movement is indistinguishable from real movement.* It is (perceptually) equivalent.

Their radical assertion was proved using a well-known phenomenon called the "waterfall effect" (or motion aftereffect) previously described by Aristotle around 350 B.C. When you stare at the water cascading from a waterfall for an extended period of time then shift your gaze to a static rock on the shore, that rock appears to be moving upward. The same thing can be seen when the wheels of a car or bicycle have been spinning at a certain rate for a length of time. After looking away, the wheel can appear to spin in the opposite direction. This is real movement in the real world, but the eye and the brain report otherwise. Wertheimer, Koffka, and Köhler repeated these experiments using a spinning spiral graphic rotating at a constant speed in a clockwise direction (like water spiraling down a drain) [↘]. This spinning was presented for a set time then paused. When paused, the spiral appeared to move in the opposite direction. Instead of spiraling inward, the static spiral appeared to expand. The effect was more powerful depending on the length of exposure.

This same experiment was repeated with the aid of the tachistoscope. In place of a physically spinning spiral, subjects were exposed to a sequence of static graphic frames of the same spiral "spinning." The psychologists took care to ensure that the graphic and its presentation to the experiment's subjects was as parallel as possible and that subjects were unaware of whether they were seeing real or apparent movement. They were then asked to describe the motion aftereffect that resulted from each. Was it stronger after watching the first (spinning) graphic or after being exposed to a series of still frames one after the other? Did the aftereffect last longer in one instance?

Subjects overwhelmingly reported that either they could detect no difference, or even that the effect was stronger after being exposed to the apparent motion produced by discrete frames. Further, subjects failed to identify which was real movement and which was apparent. According to their senses, the two types were indistinguishable. Wertheimer and his colleagues concluded that apparent movement is a perceptual fact. It's not an illusion or a trick. Apparent movement is identical in your mind, brain, and eye to real movement. They published a short paper of their findings, which received both considerable attention and skepticism at the time.

* * *

So, this guy [↑] is running, right? He doesn't have many pixels to do his running, however. He's also composed of only a few discrete frames and each looks remarkably abstract. It's almost unbelievable—in any one frame, it looks more like he's doing a little dance than running. Where is his head? Why does his eight-pixel body turn like that? Anyway, when these remarkably abstract moments are put together, and in this particular order, the brain automatically invents the glue in-between and conveys the distinct, unmistakable sensation of a small figure running.

You've probably heard the phrase "The whole is greater than the sum of its parts." And that would seem to describe what's going on with the running man above. However, according to this tight-knit group of German psychologists that statement is not quite true. They suggest that we perceive the world in organized wholes, not in parts at all. These wholes are our primary sense reports—they are not contingent on, nor comprised of elementary sensations. So, then, the whole isn't greater than the sum of its parts at all, it's simply different from the sum of its parts. With the running man, we perceive him as one figure moving, built up as much from the spaces and timing between the frames as the frames themselves. It's not a sum, even one that adds up to too much, but rather a *new, distinct, dynamic, and inseparable whole.*

WHOLE ≠ PART + PART + PART + PART

Then the whole is a new thing [↑], completely separate from any sum of its parts. In fact, Wertheimer and crew suggested that the new whole doesn't even have parts—it cannot be reduced or atomized into a series of bits. This whole, the running man, is *a thing in itself,* and, importantly, the whole comes before. You perceive the world first as wholes. This idea was a radical break from the dominant scientific rationalism that worked to explain a given reality by analyzing the pieces that construct it: principles were discovered and stacked brick by brick, bean by bean, to produce a coherent account. Instead, for Wertheimer and friends, the parts are rendered secondary. What matters are wholes, their specific organization—a set of relations, a particular configuration, a form, a shape, a gestalt.

Gestalt doesn't translate readily into English, but it has become a fundamental principle in graphic design. In Switzerland, the *activity of designing* is known as *gestalten*, which can mean "form-giving" or "whole-making," and this is different from the German word for designing, *entwerfen*. Gestalt psychology has been hotly contested within the field in the meantime, but it has been embraced within the instruction and body of graphic design, aided by individuals—conduits—who channeled this thinking directly from the source into art and design. Several of these appear later in the course.

Optical illusions trade in Gestalt psychology and offer a way to understand how it applies to graphic form. Here are two lines with arrows at either end [↘], one set pointing in and the other out. Which line is longer?

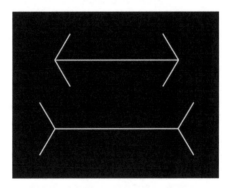

Or, this [↘].

It's a visual illusion of a vase, which also shows two faces, and was first described by Danish psychologist Edgar Rubin in 1915 while unpacking how our brain distinguishes figure and ground in the visual field. In this arrangement, the positive form of the vase carries within its negative space the silhouettes of two human faces in profile. As you read the graphic it appears first as a vase, but when attention is shifted to the negative spaces another reading comes forward. The figure-ground relation becomes fuzzy and the form flips back and forth at the mercy of our own perceptual capacities. This is neither as tricky nor trivial as it might seem.

What's achieved in both cases is done through careful organization of graphic form, and close consideration of the internal relationships. In the first illusion, the Gestalt principle of Common Fate leads a viewer to perceptually stretch the bottom line based on the direction of its arrow heads. The second uses the perceptual default of seeing recognizable shapes to register first a vase and then two faces. Either can be exaggerated or reduced depending on exactly how it is rendered [↙].

Balance, shape, line, and positive and negative spaces are all motivated to realize the essentially equal balance between possible readings. Similar techniques and attention to graphic form are used to encode visual messages of all varieties, from corporate logos to public signage. This logo [↘], for example, embeds a forward facing arrow produced by the negative space between the "E" and the "x."

It uses a similar approach to figure and ground as the vase-face, and the result makes it easily recognizable. Or take the octagonal form of a stop sign which together with its all-caps sans serif typography, red ground, and white border, creates a sign whose visual form—its wholeness or gestalt: is more important than its literal message.

This is a course in graphic design, but it also carries a secondary subject—Gestalt psychology. We will cover how that other body of knowledge connects to the discipline of graphic design, how it's been used in the language, and how its ideas have been incorporated directly, first in Western Europe, then in the United States, and how it spread across the world, meeting similar ideas developed separately in other places. A few characters will be introduced along the way, including Max Bill, Rudolf Arnheim, George Corrin, Donis Dondis, Susan Kare, and György Kepes. These form a partial, and anecdotally assembled, constellation of examples, each of whose work helped further the insights of a vacationing psychologist fascinated by a railroad crossing sign.

A Few Forms

Here's Max Bill [↑]. He's drawing some remarkably neat circles on the chalkboard. This image gives me some—perhaps false—insight into Bill's character, as someone who would be able to draw such a precise circle again and again on the chalkboard in overlapping configurations. Bill was born in 1908, in Switzerland, and studied architecture. He identified as an architect and, in fact, designed many buildings, but he was also a graphic designer. He was also an industrial designer. He was also an artist and a teacher and a writer. Bill was a generalist who didn't make crisp distinctions between design practices—he let the projects and the work lead. I like that aspect of his practice.

Here is Bill sitting at his drafting table [↑] with a pair of French curves, designing a spoon. And here [↓] he's working on a sculpture.

His sculptures were often commissioned for public spaces and took the shape of three-dimensional, complex geometric forms, like Möbius strips, modified spheres, Klein bottles, and other gestalt forms. Bill was a modernist, meaning that he adopted a brand-new visual vocabulary that was in step with the way the world was changing around him; he had a desire for new forms that addressed new problems, never defaulting to what existed previously, but rather reinventing each time, obeying poet Ezra Pound's ur-modernist command to "make it new."

Bill both designed exhibitions and mounted exhibitions of his own graphic works, sculptures, and design projects. And while his work looks utterly rational, even calculated, he was not essentially a rationalist. Bill didn't believe in ideal systems that exist beyond the scope of what you perceive. He was a committed empiricist and believed in everyday experience— what you perceive to exist is more important than what may actually exist. This thinking was very much in line with Gestalt psychologists who privileged relations between objects over the objects themselves. He would have first intersected with Gestalt psychology when he attended the Bauhaus between 1927 and 1929.

BAUHAUS: Experimental, influential, and itinerant German art school which operated between 1919 and 1933. Students at the Bauhaus (literally "building house") completed a common foundation year and then enrolled in a discipline-specific workshop, such as furniture design, ceramics, or wall-painting. The workshops were oriented towards industrial application and combined hands-on collective and individual work with theoretical instruction. This merging of art and craft, theory and practice, design and industry, has been replicated consistently since in art and design curricula around the world.

When the Bauhaus [↑] left Germany before World War II for the United States, Bill was still working in Switzerland. Together with Inge Aicher-Scholl and Otl Aicher, he developed an idea for a design school meant to follow the trajectory of the Bauhaus as a place for modern design instruction in all of the disciplines. The new school would be located in southern Germany and take its name from its setting. The Hochschule für Gestaltung Ulm, more casually known as the Ulm School, was founded in 1953. Bill was intimately involved in all aspects of the school's development. Bill designed the curriculum, was its first director, taught in the school, and even designed its building [↓].

The Ulm curriculum merged design disciplines under a comprehensive methods-based course of study distinct from the Bauhaus' hands-on workshop approach. As at the Bauhaus, Ulm students also completed a common foundation course in the first year and went on to specialize in one of several areas, including product design, visual communication, information, architecture, and later filmmaking.

Ulm also integrated itself with industry. However at Ulm, the projects included commissioned design problems such as the graphic identity for the German airline Lufthansa, product and graphic design with Braun electronics, and product, information, and graphic design for Junghans clock company. These projects inevitably involved multiple design disciplines as complex, real-world design commissions with all of their unavoidable complications. That synthesis and consistent, rational, and methodical design approach is what we know now as "The Ulm Model," and its influence has persisted since in design education. Design research was also a focus, and the school published a regular journal that collected student and faculty research projects. Ulm ran for 15 years before it closed in 1968.

Max Bill designed the curriculum, designed the building, taught, and wrote for the school's journal. But that wasn't all—he also designed furniture for the school.

This is the Ulm stool [↓].

It's a brilliant piece of design. Quite simple. The Ulm stool was meant to do several different things. It was meant to be a seat, but it was also meant to store books. It was used as a side table, a small podium. It has a round rod on the bottom for carrying it around, as it was meant to travel easily throughout the school. The stool had a group of functions that was recognized in advance of the object and these functions constituted its design. This stool needed to be student-specific, to work for sitting, travel easily to classes, be toted around campus; it should work as a bookshelf, a table, and maybe even as a kind of standing platform. Given those constraints, those demands, the shape and the form emerged almost naturally. Here [↓] it is propped on its side on a table, being used as a lectern by Bill.

Bill designed watches, timers, and wall and alarm clocks for the German manufacturer Junghans. Here [↓] is a watch face that I particularly like.

I think this has something in common with the Ulm stool. The watch needed to realize several functions. It should work as a regular 12-hour watch, but also indicate the date. It should mark the seconds and have both stopwatch timer and lap functions. Bill designed the watch face in a way that resolves these somewhat competing desires and renders them as a single coherent gestalt. Looking at the watch, you aren't immediately aware of its distinct functions. The date is shown as two digits replacing the "3" on the hour dial, the stop-watch is composed of two same-sized circles, and seconds are also marked in increments of five at the outermost edge of the face. The visual language of these is consistent—the type is all the same weight and in only two sizes, the hands are delicate, the tick marks are also equivalently weighted. The result merges the discrete functions into one clear whole.

Here is a clock which I think does it even more eloquently [↙].

It's a Junghans kitchen clock. A clock on the kitchen wall has different demands than one on a wrist, so Bill removed the second hand. In its place, he included a standard 60-minute kitchen timer. The kitchen timer looks like a kitchen timer, with a familiar dial marked out in five-minute increments and tick marks for minutes. The timer's indicator is also how it is set, and its shape invites the hand to turn it. Meanwhile, the clock face has solid black hands and very little detail. Each thing looks as expected. But then, given the desired function of this object, Bill merged the two forms, two functions, into one object by allowing each to bend and accommodate each other. This results in a particular shape that's almost generated, even secreted by the functions detailed in its brief. It's a modernist response, a new form for a new problem and it didn't look like any existing clock. Still it reads clearly as one coherent whole.

Max Bill wrote previously, if concisely, around design. In "Continuity and Change" from 1953, he writes,

> Continuity refers to that which persists. Continues to exist always in the same form. Change is the opposite of continuity. It's that which mutates, albeit within certain limits. It doesn't refer to a kind of instant transformation with no intermediate steps that you get in fairytales, for example, when a frog morphs into a prince.

He applies those two criteria to design and continues,

> The question is then to what end continuity and to what end change? Or more specifically what should be constant and what should change?

Taking as our starting point people's needs it's evident that these vary from place to place. Nevertheless, there are certain basic things that all people need: forks, knives, spoons, plates, cups, chairs, tables, beds, and other everyday objects of this kind.

There are regional variations in use, so for example in China and Japan they don't use forks but chopsticks. Chairs also take on different forms depending on where and how they're being used. But within a region there's little variation in an object's perceived purpose. Given the stability of purpose and use that doesn't change, it's continuous. One would expect a certain continuity. But just look at our cutlery and the way it is developed. It's clear that it has undergone a huge number of changes and it's hard to find a single spoon whose form is untouched by contemporary styling, never mind one defined solely by its distinct though versatile use. So we have external, artificial, stylistic changes exerting an influence over the continuity of the perceived purpose therefore regulating the continuity of the form.

Bill is making a distinction between design and styling. If the function hasn't changed, why should the form? Modern design adheres to the aphorism "form follows function," but the next sentence in the original quote is, "Where function does not change, form does not change." This is essentially what Bill is saying here when he connects this to the idea of gestalt:

> So we have external artificial stylistic changes exerting an influence over the continuity of the perceived purpose therefore regulating the continuity of the form. I'm not sure whether the desire to have a spoon for all time, which always looks the same because it is always used the same way should be put down for a striving for perfection or a striving for freedom or striving for absolutism. Or whether the spoon is continually tinkered without some irrepressible instinct for play or a desire for variation. I do however believe that the spoon is continually changing because we haven't yet found its true form, the form that corresponds to all different functions. This form depends less on some stroke of creative inspiration than it does on its purpose which is first to be defined and then comprehensively tested. From this we get a form that is provisional at first and requires patient development to become what we call gestalt. Gestalt in this sense is more than form—it embraces that which is valid and constant. I'd like to call this kind of change organic development in that it arises out of the givens of function with the proviso that when the purpose changes the gestalt does too.

He's not advocating a simple, reductive, or eternal form, but simply saying an object's design should correspond to the way that it's used, and it should resolve that use in a coherent shape. Of course, spoons exist in all sorts of different forms, in different contexts and with different functional demands. But Bill offers a useful provocation—is there or can there be one valid gestalt, a *true form* for a design problem which matches perfectly its specific functions and resolves these in one eternal whole?

In "Function and Gestalt" from 1958, Bill advances his argument. He starts with the word "function" and applies it in its strict mathematic sense, meaning something as a function of something else or one thing that depends on another variable, whose value changes based on the other variable. When you talk about an object's function, you're talking about the way in which it relates to something outside of itself. And it is exactly that relationship that you are trying to work out. It's not how it's used, which might be what we would think of as function, but rather how it relates to or, better, depends on something else. So, we could say that the function of a chair is sitting. Or the function of a pencil is writing.

The functions embedded in a design problem might be many, but those functions also need to have a coherent relationship to each other. He says,

> We can distinguish between at least two different groups of functions. The first one reveals the relations between the object and people as individuals and as a society. The second one reveals the relations between the components that make up the object and the processes by which it's produced…. All these things have to be resolved to get the correct gestalt of a certain problem.

And concludes for now,

> The more exact the definition of these functions, the clearer the requirements, then the more unified the result will be…. The result is visibly manifest as form; its unity as *gestalt*.

Assignment 1, Stop

Design an autonomous graphic form that means "Stop."

The new Stop sign must not rely on existing symbolic conventions such as an octagon or a raised hand, graphic conventions such as a slash or an X, or literal conventions such as the word "stop." This will make your task difficult, perhaps even impossible. Can a single graphic ever be autonomous, not relying on a system of differences in which to register its meaning? Keep in mind that the Stop sign is not a physical sign manufactured in steel and reflective vinyl. Instead, think of the Stop sign as more of a Stop symbol whose material support is a person's brain.

> Week 1: Explore graphic solutions by making 100 small pencil sketches, arranged ten per sheet on letter-sized paper.

> Week 2: Select the five most effective sketches, based on feedback. Render each as a black-and-white hard-line drawing on letter-sized paper. Compare notes with others on the results as a means of establishing a set of criteria for what makes a graphically successful Stop sign.

> Week 3: Based on the most successful drawings from Week 2, and incorporating relevant feedback, develop three alternative versions on letter-sized paper.

> Week 4: Produce a single, refined Stop sign.

In order to successfully fulfill this assignment, it may be necessary to cheat, strategically ignoring some of the embedded restrictions.

The Language of Visual Thinking

Rudolf Arnheim was a German who emigrated to the United States during World War II. He studied psychology at the University of Berlin under Max Wertheimer and Wolfgang Köhler. At the time Max Planck and Albert Einstein were also teaching at the school, so it was a rich moment. Psychology was part of the Department of Philosophy, and the Psychological Institute at the University of Berlin was housed on two expansive floors of the Imperial Palace. The ad hoc situation provided plenty of room for the students to setup and conduct experiments on each other. Much of the interest around the Institute was in Gestalt psychology and perception, and Arnheim was drawn to all of this. He was also interested in art and personal expression, and when he left school he began to bring the lessons of Gestalt psychology directly into the fields of art and design at schools like Sarah Lawrence College, Harvard University, and the University of Michigan, where he taught psychology and wrote about art.

Arnheim published several books which translated Gestalt psychology for the world of art and design, two of which are well-known. The first, *Art and Visual Perception* (1954), has been translated into 14 languages and remains one of the most consequential art books of the 20th century. The second was a bit less of a publishing juggernaut—*Visual Thinking* (1969) [↘].

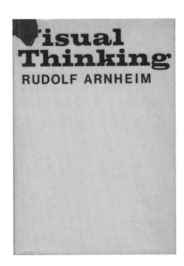

As the title suggests, it wrestles with the differences between perceiving and thinking, suggesting that they are the same thing. Arnheim writes,

Thinking, productive thinking, should happen in images.

That's visual thinking—a different kind of thinking that uses the spatial capacities of your brain to think in images and solve problems intuitively. Arnheim lays out a series of visual thinking exercises in the text by which picturing a model in your mind's eye helps to reveal parts of a problem that would not be so easily described otherwise. In one, Arnheim asks the reader to imagine a 3 × 3 × 3 cube composed of 27 individual cubes. (Basically, it's a Rubik's cube.) The cube is painted red on all sides. Now, picture the cube, turn it around, have a look and a think. How many cubes that make up that composite cube have zero sides colored red?

The correct answer is one. It's the cube at the center of the object. Second question: How many cubes are painted red on only one side? Again this requires spinning the cube in your head. (The answer is six.) How many cubes have exactly two painted red sides? (Twelve.) And how many have three painted red sides? (Eight.) Through this example, Arnheim offers a demonstration of how visual thinking can help answer such synthetic questions. The mental (that is, visual) model can be examined, interrogated. But, crucially, what is really being interrogated are the relations between the objects. It's not just turning an image around and looking at it, but also trying to understand how one thing relates to another: What are the relations? How is a thing put together? And how does it come apart?

I don't play chess, but I understand that chess players learn to hold games in their heads, entire gestalts of matches encoded as individual moves around the board. I like that idea—it seems like a variety of visual thinking. In 1929, while a student at the Bauhaus, Josef Hartwig designed a chess set, which seems to capture this idea. The Bauhaus chess set has a compelling gestalt form [↓].

How the individual pieces look relate directly to how they move: the pawns are small cubes and they move one space; the bishop is an extruded X and it moves diagonally. The knight is a complex adjusted cubic figure and it performs the up-two-and-over-one move. The castle is a larger solid cube (basically a scaled-up pawn) and it can move many spaces in one direction. You can see the game together with its rules of play, encoded into its form. It's a beautiful gestalt.

I'm now going to introduce György Kepes. For a few years Arnheim and Kepes were just a couple miles apart on Massachussets Avenue in Cambridge (Arnheim was at Harvard and Kepes at MIT). They were covering similar territory: the application of Gestalt psychology to design and art. But where Arnheim came from Gestalt psychology to art and design, Kepes came from art and design to Gestalt psychology. Kepes even designed the cover [↓] of Rudolf Arnheim's first book, *Film as Art*.

At the time, Kepes was in Berlin and working as an assistant in the design studio of László Moholy-Nagy, the Hungarian artist and Bauhaus teacher. Kepes followed Moholy to London before World War II broke out and then Chicago, where Mohloy-Nagy was invited to establish the New Bauhaus at the Institute of Design. Kepes led the course in Light and Color at the school before accepting an invitation from MIT in 1947 to establish a new program in visual design.

Here's Kepes [↑]. He was Hungarian like Moholy-Nagy. In 1967, 20 years after establishing visual design at MIT, Kepes was offered the opportunity to set up the Center for Advanced Visual Studies, an independent research organization within the university that brought together artists and scientists for large-scale collaborations. It was well-funded, Kepes was well-known, and he was a strong advocate for putting design on equal footing with other artistic practices. In a short video from the time, Kepes reveals his orientation.

> There is an obvious and sometimes fearful discrepancy between life as it is and life as it should and could be. But most of us, if we can re-instill our confidence in life, try to find ways to bridge this gap. Artists are among those that have a passionate commitment to the completeness of life. Today one doesn't need to have too much imagination, or extra sensitivity to see how the urban life we created for ourselves is not living up to its potential.

Kepes published *Language of Vision* in 1944. It calls for a new order of seeing that is appropriate for, even demanded by, the context of the world at the time. World War II had just ended, communications and travel technology were accelerating, the destructive failure of totalitarianism and war provided fertile ground for wholesale reconstruction. And Kepes made a strong plea in the book's introduction for a new kind of visual communication that would reintegrate people across cultures, space, and time. With an explicit nod to Gestalt psychology, he wrote,

> Visual communication is universal and international; it knows no limits of tongue, vocabulary, or grammar, and it can be perceived by the illiterate as well as by the literate.

And a new type of perception of the visual environment was equally important. Images and visual communications were to be decoded and assembled by the viewer in the moment. Kepes called this the "plastic formation" of images and described the process like this:

> To perceive a visual image implies the beholder's participation in a process of organization. The experience of an image is thus a creative act of integration. It's essential characteristic is that by plastic power an experience is formed into an organic whole.

Anyway, it is easy enough to pick out the ethical undertones of what Kepes is suggesting—reading the visual world is a synthetic act, and it requires individual participation rather than merely passive consumption.

In 1965, Kepes began to edit a series of design anthologies based on the ideas he wrote about in *Language of Vision*. These books are collected under the name *Vision + Value* and they work like a series of textbooks, or perhaps better, a multi-volume art and design almanac. Kepes was well-connected to many people writing about art and design at the time and he collected essays from these thinkers in the books. Rudolph Arnheim, for example, was one of the contributors. Each is populated with extensive illustrations.

Kepes didn't use the word "gestalt" prominently, but he drew upon its ideas and its imagery. And by the late 1960s, he was interested in the same issues of dynamic interrelationships within a form and how those cause it to snap together into one coherent whole. He emphasized the viewer's role in the process and the ethics of this engagement. He also addressed how internal relationships can be left unresolved, provoke anxiety, and can create a specific tension just by the position of one thing within another thing. It's as if Kepes might say, "This feels different. This means something essentially different because of where this meets that, where it's touching the edge." And, if you are drawn toward graphic design, I think you know this intuitively. That is to say, you feel what I'm describing.

Assignment 1 (adjusted), Go

Design an autonomous graphic form that means "Go."

This assignment begins in Week 2 of the Stop sign, prior to completing the final version; the task now both broadens and forks.

Two or more graphics can work together in a visual syntax to mean something that neither means on its own. Syntax describes the relations between words and dictates their positions to produce well-formed sentences in a language. Visual syntax works in a similar way, with graphics standing in for words. As "Go" means the opposite of "Stop," then the two graphics should have an opposing relation to each other. The graphics should convey their relationship immediately, intuitively, and visually to produce a very limited graphic language composed of these two symbols. For example, in a stoplight, green means "Go," and red, "Stop." Green and red are opposite colors.

Week 1: Explore graphic solutions by making 100 small pencil sketches, arranged ten per sheet on letter-sized paper.

Week 2: Select the five most effective sketches, based on feedback. Render each as a black-and-white hard-line drawing on letter-sized paper.

Week 3: Produce a single, refined Go sign.

As with the Stop sign, the Go sign must not rely on symbolic, graphic, or literal conventions. The Go sign will be directly related to, and dependent on, the form of the Stop sign.

Currently in Process

This is *A Primer of Visual Literacy* [↓].

This graphic design textbook was written by Donis A. Dondis, published by MIT Press in 1973, and is currently in its 23rd printing. It was
designed by Muriel Cooper. Cooper and Dondis were classmates at
Massachusetts College of Art in the 1950s and remained friends.
When the book was written, Dondis was teaching graphic design at
Boston University in the School of Public Communication and Cooper
was design director at MIT Press. (She would soon start teaching in
the Department of Architecture.) The book evolved from a running conversation between the two around teaching graphic design in the context
of massive changes to the media landscape. The book proposed that
in an age of mass electronic visual communication (such as television),
reading and writing images was as fundamental as reading and writing
words. Dondis ends the first chapter describing what's at stake:

> What you see is a major part of what you know, and visual literacy can help
> us to see what we see and to know what we know.

The book presents itself as a kind of extended slide lecture, or a series of lectures marked off as chapters; running texts interjected with demonstration images, in-line illustrations that work like projected illustrations. The book's pacing is deliberate and the tone is solidly didactic and incremental. Reading it feels like sitting in a classroom, in a good way.

The proximity of author and designer and their shared investment in the contents led to a subtly strange layout. The book's typography is slightly off and feels automated, with a uniformly light Univers type, consistently awkward letterspacing, and affectations such as underlines in place of italics. Turns out that the typography was a consequence of its production. At the time Muriel Cooper had set up a research unit in the basement of the MIT Press offices and was exploring the application of electric and electronic typewriters to produce camera-ready typography. This book was set on an (only) slightly more advanced system, the IBM Electronic Composer which allowed for variable-spaced typesetting in a wider range of types. The great advantage was that layouts could be created completely in-house and this resulted in a more iterative design and editing process. The disadvantage was the quality of the typesetting. This is also part of what gives the book a visual spark [↓].

elements: line, color, shape, direction, texture, scale, dimension, motion. Which elements dominate which visual statements is determined by the nature of what is being designed or, in the case of nature, what exists. But when we define painting elementally as tonal, filled with

When I've used this book in teaching (which is often), I ask students: Why does the cover look like it does? It looks to me like writing, or some kind of coded message. What does it say?

I've received a few almost-plausible suggestions over the years to explain the six rows of graphic shapes, which look to me like basic letterforms. After at least seven years of asking this question, the answer dawned on me. What the cover is "saying" cannot be articulated in English or any other written language. The six rows run through permutations of three primary visual forms borrowed from the Bauhaus. Square, circle, and triangle outlines repeat on each row with lines of each shape omitted. This is not a written message, it is a visual message. The fact that it took me so long to read this cover should make me consider spending more time absorbing the book's lessons.

The book uses Gestalt psychology as a foundation. Cooper had been a fellow at the Center for Advanced Visual Studies when György Kepes was the director. Walter Gropius, former head of the Bauhaus, was leading the graduate design school at Harvard at the time and Gestalt psychology factored directly into the architecture and design curriculum. Rudolf Arnheim was nearby at Harvard. Artist Josef Albers, a Gestaltist who also emigrated from the Bauhaus, was head of the Yale University School of Art. Gestalt psychology and its application to design was not a distant concept and Dondis and Cooper embraced it directly. Page 21 (from Chapter 2, "Composition: The Syntactical Guidelines for Visual Literacy") starts like this:

> Gestalt psychology has contributed valuable research and experimentation in the area of perception, collecting data and searching the significance of visual patterns, as well as finding how the human organism sees and organizes visual input and articulates visual output. Together, the physical and the psychological are relative and not absolute. Every visual pattern has a dynamic quality that cannot be defined intellectually, emo-tionally, or mechanically by size or direction or shape or distance. These stimuli are only static measurements, but the psychophysical forces they set off, like those of any stimuli, modify space and arrange or derange balance. Together they create the perception of a design or an environment or a thing.

And then comes the best part, and also, refreshingly, the strangest way to say it:

> All things visual are not just something that happens out there. They are visual events, total occurrences, actions that incorporate the reaction into the whole.

The chapter continues to develop the idea of a visual syntax, built up by the viewer and constructed from the dynamic relationships between the graphic forms. Graphic signs always indicate a relation to another graphic sign, and these dynamic relations constitute whole messages, the building blocks of what Dondis would call a "visual language." The context of one symbol makes it easier to read the other, and meaning exists not in either alone, but rather in the gap between the two.

I've often found students are hungry for rules to graphic design. And although I don't believe such rules exist, I do like that *A Primer* at least makes a few attempts. On occasion, a generous, solicitous offering of something concrete is just what's called for in place of the harder answer that these universal rules simply don't exist. For example, a discussion on balance shows what's being described and offers more than one illustration per point. This is pretty different from a text where illustrations are used as ballast to support an argument. *A Primer of Visual Literacy* wants to teach, not convince, its reader.

For example, the Gestalt principle of *Prägnanz* (definitiveness, resolution, simplicity) is presented. It's a furry concept but handled with clarity and copious illustration. Some relationships—graphic relationships—are more salient, more assured, more resolved than others. And so at the bottom of the page [↘] are two rows of figures. The top row are clearly recognized as the regular geometric figures of the square, triangle, and circle.

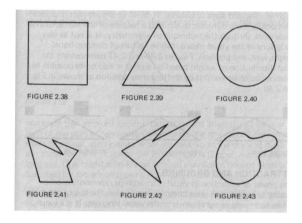

FIGURE 2.38   FIGURE 2.39   FIGURE 2.40

FIGURE 2.41   FIGURE 2.42   FIGURE 2.43

The second row has three considerably more ambiguous (and less easily named) figures. The top represents "good" *Prägnanz*, or simple, coherent, specific forms. The bottom is the opposite. By offering both example and counter-example, the simple point is generously explained.

A Primer of Visual Literacy is premised on the existence of a second language outside of spoken or written communication. This language is visual and simultaneous rather than literal and sequential. It is both read and written; it has a vocabulary, a grammar, a syntax, even meaning. On page 44, the trio of primary forms [↓] from the cover reappear.

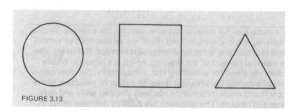

FIGURE 3.13

This time the square, triangle, and circle are pushed into service to convey the meanings of specific shapes. Dondis is straight and authoritative, if not entirely convincing:

> The square has associated to it dullness, honesty, and workmanlike meaning; the triangle, action, conflict, tension; the circle, endlessness, warmth, protection.

* * *

This is a scan of my wristwatch from 2009 [↓].

It was the result of an invitation extended to Dexter Sinister to participate in an exhibition in New York. Instead of being represented in the show itself, we suggested producing a publicity image—a piece of graphic design—for the show. And we would treat this self-assignment with the same degree of attention as any other artwork.

The exhibition was about the changing physical landscape of New York City and was oriented around a map showing where avant-garde figures at the leading edge of the arts lived in the city during the 20th century. The show was essentially about time, or that's where we took it, and this is why we decided to scan a watch. We produced the image by scanning my watch at 1200 dots per inch. At this high resolution, the scanning head is moving slower than the second hand on the watch, and as a result, in the image the second hand appears to bend [↓] as it moves.

Here's another watch face. This one manifested from an invitation to redesign the display of the Casio F91, a very common digital wristwatch. It was an art project organized by Halmos in New York, where multiples were produced for sale at a reasonable price. When Dexter Sinister got this commission, I immediately thought we should do a digital translation of the analog watch scan—what would that look like?

I typed "Dexter Sinister digital watch scan" into Google and shockingly, the internet conjured this [↑] image. Years later I met Federico Antonini, the Italian graphic designer and artist who produced it. He took his own digital wristwatch, put it on the scanner, and also scanned it at a very high dpi. In his image you see the red, green, and blue of the liquid crystal display. So, we could not do this since it had already been done. We decided to work in reverse. Instead of slowing down the scanner or image-making apparatus, we would slow down the display of time across the face of the watch.

Digital watches typically use a quartz crystal that, when electricity is introduced, resonates at a certain frequency and drives the watch. Quartz is used because it has a very stable resonant frequency and this keeps it running at the correct rate. The display moves across the face left to right, drawing each number segment by segment over time. (It takes time to tell the time.) The existing Casio F91 watches already drew each segment at different moments, but it all happens too fast to visually register. A new circuit board—the watch's brain—was designed and installed which would slow down the left-to-right drawing, producing a slowed-down display as a kind of inverted watch scan. The new watch relies on the Gestalt principle of being able to hold a sequence of images in your head even if it's distended in time.

Here's the finished product [↑]. Because the digital display is slowed down and it draws left to right, at any one moment the watch shows only part of the current time. The display speed is adjustable, however, and you're instructed to set the display as slow as possible so that you can still read the time. This should mark the limits of your perception, and it should be at the tipping point where the time is no longer legible.

These two projects are related, superficially by both being watch face design projects, but more emphatically they both have to do with the holding of a temporal sequence in your head over time as one gestalt— like a melody, or a sequence of discrete frames in a film.

* * *

Watch faces and temporal displays are something graphic designers are often tasked with. In 1984, the Apple Macintosh was introduced. It was a personal, portable computer driven by a one-button mouse and the first consumer-facing graphic user interface. There was no existing visual precedent for communicating the novel user interactions of the powerful new machine, and so everything had to be invented from scratch.

Susan Kare [↑] is a designer based in San Francisco. She was the designer of the original visual language for the Macintosh interface. Kare was invited by Apple engineer Bill Atkinson and it seems she arrived to the project with very few preconceptions.

One interaction problem which needed to be solved with graphic design was called "perceived responsiveness"—something that lets you know the computer is thinking. The first Macintosh was small and slow. You turned it on, booted it up from a floppy disk, and waited for a while, and you needed to know that you needed to wait.

Whenever the computer processor was busy, the user needed to be reassured that the computer was indeed working. This "wait cursor" was mission-critical for the user experience. The animated icon that Kare designed was a wristwatch [↘] whose hands moved slowly round in fifteen-minute increments to indicate that something was happening.

There were several other wait cursors in that original system software which were used in different scenarios [↓]. These included a hand with counting fingers, a slowly spinning planet Earth, a rotating Yin Yang symbol as some kind of Zen everything's-always-in-progress cursor, an hourglass, and the MPW cursor, which looked unnervingly like the symbol for a nuclear hazard.

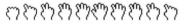

2128 Counting Fingers

2130 Zen Cursor

2129 Earth Cursor

2131 MPW Cursor

When Steve Jobs left Apple to set up NeXT Computer, Inc., Kare joined him to become the lead designer of the new software. The NeXT was a considerably more powerful computer with a more complicated interface. The simple watch cursor was discontinued and replaced with a rotating, spinning, gradated color wheel. This disk graphic was ungenerously christened the "spinning beach ball of death" [↙] by users who worried that their system had frozen whenever the ominous yet colorful graphic appeared.

Now, spinning beachballs have almost nothing to do with waiting, but this is the power of both context and repetition. It is now a recognizable graphic idea, a visual shorthand for waiting, invented out of thin air, and also only one of many possible answers.

Assignment 2, Wait

Design an animated graphic that means "Wait."

This is a new assignment, not a continuation of Assignment 1. Where the Stop and Go signs were static symbols, the Wait graphic is dynamic, an animation designed for an electronic screen.

Week 1: Begin by looking at a range of animated wait graphics. Prepare ten letter-sized sheets of pencil sketches to develop ideas. The number of alternatives is open, but fill these pages with alternatives.

Week 2: Building on your pencil sketches, draw your ideas on a computer as a series of discrete frames in an animation. Assemble the frames into a moving graphic. Prepare at least three alternatives.

Week 3: Based on feedback, select one animation from Week 2 and prepare a final Wait graphic at both 400 × 400 pixels and 40 × 40 pixels. The smaller version can be adjusted from the larger to account for its low resolution. The final product is two animated files.

What does your computer show when the system is busy? The "spinning beach ball of death" is a small animated graphic which comprises a rotating rainbow pinwheel. The animation that displays when loading new posts in the infinite scroll of Instagram is another example. Another is the animated ellipsis of Apple Messages. These graphics are called perceived responsiveness icons and indicate "in process," "busy," or "thinking."

After Effects

I like to talk about Italian artist and designer Bruno Munari, hold him up as a model, because of the general nature of his practice, which ignored boundaries between the various kinds of work he was engaged in. Munari made graphic design, sculptures, paintings, exhibitions. He lectured, he taught, and he wrote. In one text from about 1964, "A Language of Signs and Symbols?", Munari offers up his own primer on visual literacy, although typically, it has his touch of the absurd. Like Dondis, Munari is describing coherent sets of symbols with grammar, vocabulary, structure. These include electrical schematics, road signs, and hobo symbols [↓].

Hobo symbols are used to mark places, for example, along a freight train route, to indicate what may or may not be available in a town or area or what kind of people and reception to expect somewhere—helpful tips for the next traveler. The top left one is a sleepy town. The two diamonds next to each other indicate "go slow." One that actually looks like what it means is the armed man. The triangle actually looks terrified. The bent arrow for a storm is an interesting choice. Look at the symbol for hostility; that would be a hard assignment. These are icons that might be written along a well-worn hobo route, on train cars, or on a fence. They were meant to be read only by this self-selected group (tramps, hobos, vagabonds) that has decided to live this way and to adopt this visual language.

Symbols could be combined. For example, here [↙] we see armed man plus fierce dog. And then this one [↘], which looks like a face and it combines symbols from three sets to convey its message: "I am in a narrow place between rain and snow, please help."

This work is typical Munari—it is funny, it's curious, it's synthetic, and it's visual. He'd have called it "design research."

At the same time, Munari was also pursuing research into primary geometric shapes, and he published a set of three small books called *The Triangle*, *The Circle*, and *The Square*. *The Triangle* takes that simple form and traces it through an idiosyncratic collection of triangular things that had caught his eye [↓], triangles that have some bearing on his design practice.

  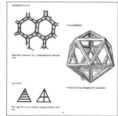

A figure by French artist and designer Sonia Delaunay wears a triangular skirt; a decorative element drawn with a compass sits on a triangle base; or a snowflake seen under a microscopic structure revealing its internal three-part structure; the Hittite signs for a city and for a king are both triangles in that ancient writing system; the Mercedes-Benz logo is a circle divided by three. Each image includes a short caption. Munari uses this simple formal device, a triangle, to hop across gaps in time and in culture. The result is a book of design research driven by a visual form which motivates that form as a tool to navigate across wide categorical registers. Deep history and contemporary graphics are presented equivalently, and this equivalence allows an associative and lateral way of looking.

There are serious limitations to this approach, but for Munari it offered a way to keep his practice moving, always on to the next thing. This directed movement is particularly necessary in a design practice, where clients, deadlines, and technical constraints often conspire to assert their demands. Designers need their own inner compass or may quickly find themselves blown off course.

Meanwhile, Munari continued. In 1969, he published *Look Into My Eyes*. It's a square-format children's book that is still in print. The eyes and mouth are cut out, so that the loose pages are meant to act as masks. But stack the pages in any order and new eyes appear, one face showing through to the other [↓]. It's a rich inventory of faces and also a formal study of possibilities.

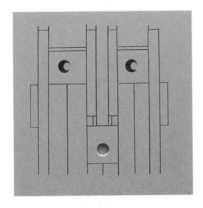 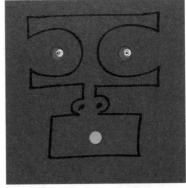

Munari described his *Useless Machines* as vehicles for understanding transformations. They are constellations of small objects connected discreetly by string, hung, and in perpetual motion and constant self-rearranging. They're not decorative objects, instead they're meant to be contemplative, even didactic, models for considering how one form moves into another. Munari [↓] made *Useless Machines* for 50 years and they were central to his practice. He even starts the preface to *Design as Art* from 1966 by introducing himself this way:

> Lots of people know me as, "You know, the man who made the useless machines."

And continues,

> ... even today I still occasionally get asked one of these objects which I designed and made about 1933. That was the time when the movement called the *novecento italiano* ruled the roost with its high court of super serious masters and all the art magazines spoke of nothing else but their grand artistic productions, and everyone laughed at me and my useless machines. They laughed all the harder because my machines were made of cardboard painted in plain colors, sometimes a glass bubble, while the whole thing was held together with the frailest of wooden rods and bits of thread.

The useless machines [↓], according to Munari, diagram an internal logic which defines the relationships between their parts. These were not three-dimensional pictures of things found in nature, but rather models of the underlying structures of the natural world.

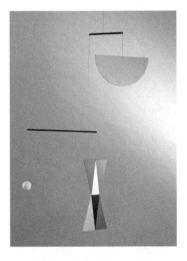

There's a long-exposure photograph [↓] of a useless machine in Munari's small booklet from 1962 called *Visual Research.* That picture reveals the composite form as an integral constellation over time.

Macchina inutile in movimento.

Concave-Convex is another series of small, dynamic sculptures he described as "by-products" of the useless machines. The construction is simple. Starting from a single square piece of wire mesh screen, find the midpoint of one side. Bring the opposite corner carefully to meet this point and secure it with fine wire. Repeat using another side. The result is a beautiful, complex three-dimensional form which is hung from the ceiling by a string. The object, however elegant, isn't the point. Rather, what matters is the constantly shifting shadow that it casts on the wall [↓].

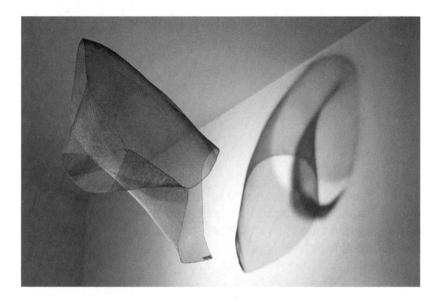

In *Design as Art*, he writes,

> The shadow projected looks like a drawing, with an effect not unlike that of an old print, but when it is in motion it gives beautiful moiré effects that appear and dissolve like a cloud.

It's an object whose purpose is to produce this changing set of images that have an internal structural logic one to the next. And the shapes are surprisingly complex as they appear on the wall. The shadows include interference, or moiré, patterns, which result from two or more layers of the screen material overlaying each other.

MOIRÉ: Graphic interference patterns produced from the imposition of two repeating screens with regular patterns. As screens of either different frequencies, different sizes, or different rotations are moved in relation to each other, the visual effect moves into and out of phase, becoming less and more intense in a predictable sequence. The length of the phase varies with relative density, scale, and rotation.

That interference pattern then became a new subject for a series of investigations. For Munari, one thing always led to another. Here is a graduated dot screen [↓]. And here [↘] is the same pattern duplicated, rotated, and superimposed on itself to produce a moiré.

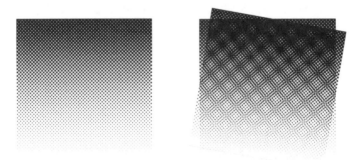

Munari's independent research ended up applied as book covers for publishers Einaudi and Bompiani, as silkscreen prints, and he also wrote about the phenomenon in an article called "Notes for An Exploration into the World of Moiré." [↓]

He writes,

> There are unexplored zones where artists have not yet ventured to carry out their experiments. Of course, this also depends on the character of the artists, and by artists I mean not only painters but all those in the graphic arts and all those concerned with visual art. Indeed, there are artists who've been painting horses all their lives and for them the idea of painting a zebra would be so bold as to induce them to meditate for years before facing that problem.

His humor comes through. He continues,

> Other artists instead are curious by nature, they investigate, they experiment, and they're satisfied only when they are the first to venture into unexplored zones where no one has been before or where everyone had been without seeing anything. From that moment on everyone sees. As I see it this is the artist's job, especially today when science and technology have provided us with such formidable means.

And finally, he ends,

> This exploration into the world of moiré is only a glance through a peephole on a February morning in 1962. And already anyone can see what is inside, how the screens are transformed, what forms take shape, irregular forms free from extreme severity, modulations of a certain element repeated at constant distances overlaid with barely perceptible angles or even angles of 44 degrees off center by a few tenths of a millimeter. Its surfaces barely varied.

New technology was often a research site for Munari and when the Rank Xerox black-and-white photocopier arrived in 1967, he was excited by its possibilities for image-making, and by the fact that you could do it yourself. He approached the machine as he did many other subjects, as if no one had been there before. What he made was singular—nobody else could or would have done it. These open-ended set of works are called the "Original Xerographies."

The Xerox was designed to reproduce exact copies one after the other. Instead, he used a collection of prepared abstracted graphic images (dot patterns, textures, shapes) prepared on clear acetate, and collaged them together on the bed of the photocopier in a specific arrangement and pressed the Copy button. Either happy or unhappy with the result, he rearranged and pressed Copy again. But these weren't copies at all, they were originals, one-time records of a particular arrangement at a particular time. He exaggerated this by running sheets back through the machine and overprinting, using moiré patterns, rotating, bending, crushing, and otherwise manipulating the raw materials to make unique, unrepeatable prints. An "original" copy is a contradiction in terms, but this is exactly what Munari produced—he turned the machine against itself and made it bleed poetry. They're beautiful and also somehow impossible. Here's one [↓].

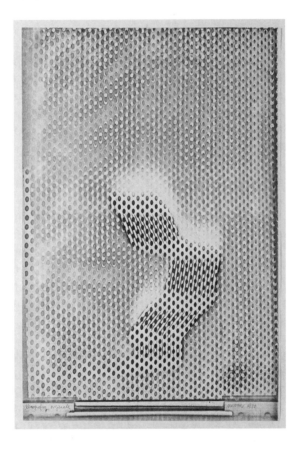

Munari incorporated the machines into his exhibitions. His first in the United States was at Howard Wise Gallery on 57th Street in New York City. On the opening night, the gallery was ready, poised to sell Munari's work, which was available in America for the first time. Instead, Munari set up a Xerox machine at the entrance, where he produced original Xeroxes, giving away his work to visitors. It wasn't meant to be seen as a performance, it was simply how Munari wanted to invite people into the show. But I don't imagine Howard Wise was amused. It was Munari's last exhibition at the gallery.

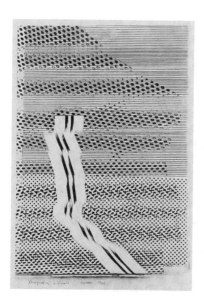
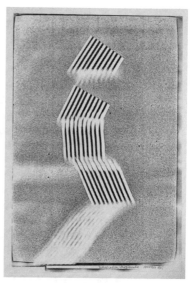

Munari continued his experiments. These two [↖] [↗] were produced by dragging a graphic form across the scanning bed as the copy was being made. The final print records these movements as an unrepeatable Xerox copy.

He also published—not because he was interested in reinforcing his own artistic authority, but rather to crack open this world so everyone can see—instructions, or guidelines, for how to make these yourself; for how you might take a diagonal grid and arrange it with a horizontal set of lines, and move them around, how you move the things in a certain way or twist them. This is a kind of recipe [↓]:

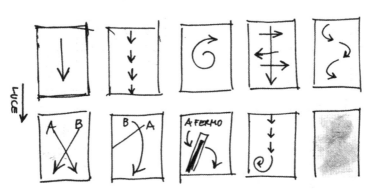

At the same time, he was also studying graphic textures. Here's one
produced by the superimposition of two simpler graphic patterns [↙].

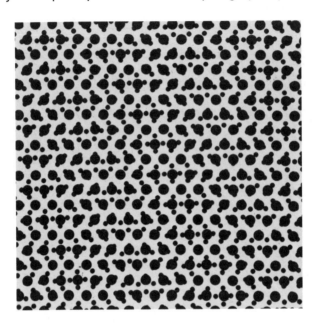

And this related texture from 1960 of "simultaneous movement" [↙]:

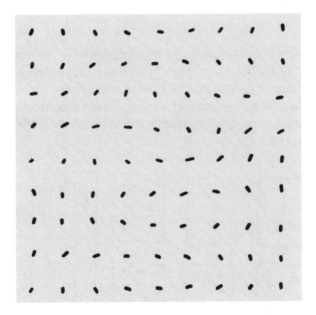

In this simple graphic, Munari had a pretty grand agenda:

This is a drawing that makes sense of how the world works now.

He was trying to understand the probabilistic machinery behind quantum mechanics, a way of understanding the basic structure of the world as a combined set of probabilities, so many individual pieces in constant motion. Looking at this drawing, there's nowhere for the eye to rest. It's in constant motion—as likely to land on one as the other.

He wasn't always working so analytically. This [↙] is a set of works called *Forchette*, or *Forks*. He made these first in an Italian restaurant in New York waiting for his food to arrive, entertaining himself (although not likely the restaurant owner). Since then, the forks have been reproduced and manufactured. They've become a set of drawings and then a book. Here's a fork smoking a cigarette [↘].

Around this time, Munari was also working for Olivetti, the Italian typewriter, adding machine, and electronics company. Olivetti had an ambitious design commissioning program and considered it part of their corporate responsibility to invite artists to work on design projects to inject artists' particular, alternative points of view into society at large. One of these commissions went to an architect, Carlo Scarpa, to design the Olivetti showroom in Venice on the corner of the Piazza San Marco in the city center. The shop was small, refined, and beautiful, presenting Olivetti's products in a jewel-box setting—surely it was the Apple Store of its day.

Since working with Olivetti, Munari was increasingly interested in computers, making works of art that engaged the then-new concept of computer programming. Munari proposed to Olivetti to make an art exhibition inside their Milan and Venice showrooms. The show would present the work of two young Italian design collectives, Gruppo T and Gruppo N, together with some of his own work, and the work of designer Enzo Mari.

Here is the showroom in Venice [↓].

The exhibition was called *Arte Programmata* (Programmed Art) and the catalogue's introductory essay by Umberto Eco describes,

> We can speak of programmed art and admire the kinetic sculptures that a man of the coming future would install in his house in place of the old prints or modern masterpieces reproduced, and if someone should observe this is not painting or even sculpture it should be of no concern.

Eco continues to describe the qualities of these works. They are produced in multiple—there is never a unique work. They are the scale of tabletop consumer products and are meant to be engaged on a one-to-one basis. They move: many use motors, lights, or even chemicals. Each is governed by a script, a plan of possible arrangements. Every work is constantly changing, although within a constrained set of possible arrangements, defined as the artwork's "program."

The programmed art of these young artist collectives worked with the metaphor of computer programming making artworks that followed scripts to produce a constantly changing form. These used motors, fluids, magnets, and electricity in place of actual computers. The artists (they actually called themselves "visual operators") also had something of a social agenda behind their work, insisting on the production not of unique art objects, but rather of designed multiples produced in open-ended editions. The artists believed that these artworks-as-con-sumer-products might circulate in society and inject artistic thinking and specific, new, challenging points of view. Here is the catalog cover [↙].

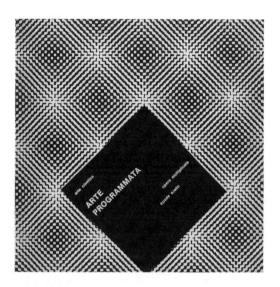

They also insisted that "program" had several related meanings which shifted in scale from the instructions to perform a set of calculations on a personal computer, all the way up to the idea of a social program, or a kind of script or plan for how a society might evolve more humanely than it might under the torqued incentives of capitalism.

Munari and Eco worked on other projects, including Munari's design for Eco's *Opera aperta* (*The Open Work*) [↑], published around the same time. *Opera aperta* is a lively collection of essays in art criticism that lobbies for artworks whose end states are unknown; works that have multiple points of entry and, most importantly, don't dictate any single view, or particular interaction at any one time. These ideas were directly embedded in the exhibition *Arte Programmata*.

Here is Munari with his own sculpture [↑] that was included in the show. It's a column of striped transparent spheres resting on top of a motor, so that when one spins, the others also spin, creating a shifting and abstract pattern. And then, here's Gruppo T [↓], five artists who came out of the Brera Academy in Milan and worked collectively. (The "T" in Gruppo T stood for "time"!)

And here's one of the works in the show from Gruppo T. It's called *Fluid Structuring* [↘] and presents a clear plastic band that moves into continuously changing folded arrangements using a motor in its base and the resistance of the material to create a constantly morphing sculpture.

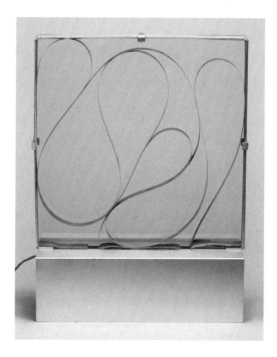

All of these works required the close participation and observation of the viewer, to register how they change over time.

That wasn't nearly all Munari was up to in the mid-1960s. He also set up a small film studio north of Milan, near Como, with director Marcello Piccardo. The studio was called Monte Olimpino, and Munari used it to make short experimental research films. One such film is *Tempo nel Tempo* (Time in Time), made in 1964 and in collaboration with the Polytechnic of Milan. The film records an acrobat performing a backflip. The acrobat poises himself on a red cube then launches into the flip while the soundtrack of a ticking watch in realtime plays. Next, this footage, shot with a very high-shutter-speed camera, is slowed way down and stretched to last the rest of the film's running length of 3 minutes, 26 seconds. As you watch, you already know what's coming next (the acrobat will complete his backflip), but you don't know exactly what the next frame will look like. In slow motion, surprisingly strange body positions appear at any one moment.

Here is a still from *Tempo nel Tempo* (Time in Time) [↓].

Another Munari work again addresses a form that constantly changes. The *X Hour Clock* from 1963 has hands made of transparent acrylic semicircles which overlay each other to create a changing graphic image.

Hour, minute, second, and am/pm hands were each fitted with different colors (yellow, blue, red, green) so as the clock proceeded through the day, it also produced an evolving color composition. Depending on when you check, the time looks like this [↙]. Or this [↘].

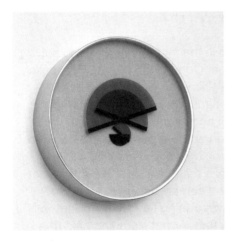 

This clock was made as a multiple, manufactured by Danese Milano, and launched in their showroom, where Munari installed an assembly of

24 *X Hour* clocks [↓], each set to a different time zone.

At the time, Munari was also making a series of paintings called *Negative-Positive*. In the series, Munari directly addressed Gestalt theories of perception, attempting to create images that are equal parts figure and ground. He made a related film called *After Effects*, which reproduced Max Wertheimer's spinning spiral disk apparent motion experiment together with a few other Gestalt perceptual tests. A *Negative-Positive* painting [↙] feels less like an expressive painting than it does like a research exercise or experiment. Likewise, *After Effects* is certainly not a narrative film, not a documentary film, not even an abstract film. It's more of a tool, a model, even a research instrument. The same could be said of his *Polariscope* [↘] from the same time.

The *Polariscope* was a fairly small steel box which housed a polarized light filter which blocks wavelengths of light arriving at a specific angle. When the filter is turned 90 degrees, the light passes through. Munari's machine allowed him to experiment with the many visual effects the filter could produce. He then used the technique for slide projections, light works, and design projects.

Here's a view through the *Polariscope* [↙] and a book cover designed with the machine [↘].

Here's the last project I'll talk about today. Munari designed it in 1965 and it was also produced by Danese Milano. It's a multiple artwork, a petite steel cube with four aluminum cones, each painted half red and half green. It was designed with a motor, gears, and a specific script which dictated that each cone spins at a specific speed [↙].

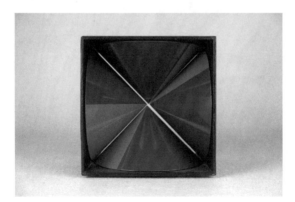

The result is a constantly changing face that moved from entirely green to entirely red over the course of 18 minutes. The object was called the *Tetracono* and it was designed to show "forms in the process of becoming."

Assignment 3, RGB v. CMYK

Design a collection of animated, printed, and physical graphics which articulate the differences between RGB and CMYK color models.

This is a design research project. It is considerably more open-ended and self-directed than the previous two assignments. The goal is to understand the fundamental distinction between additive and subtractive color, as manifest by RGB and CMYK color models.

Week 1: Starting in a library, find books that detail the distinctions between the two color models. Let the selection of books help to guide the next steps in the research process. Continue the research online. Prepare a five-minute presentation to be shown in Week 2 which concisely identifies the differences between RGB and CMYK color.

Week 2: The most effective way to learn about color is by directly making it and looking at it. Therefore, proceed empirically, comparing printed colors to screen colors. For example, what happens when you print the brightest on-screen green and compare the printed sheet to the glowing screen?

Using these practical experiments as a guide, refine the inquiry to one part of this broad problem. For example, investigate how printed ink fades over time and discover if there is a corollary effect on screen. Or focus only on the color green which is tricky to render in both models. Or investigate sub-pixels on-screen and halftone dot patterns on the printed page. From there explore the limits of what either system can handle. All of these experiments are just that, hands-on experiments. This is a design research project where thinking and making are collapsed into one fluid activity.

Weeks 3–4: The final products of this assignment are variable and completely open. Where the previous assignments were prescribed and directed, the working method for this project should more accurately reflect the lateral thinking and meandering processes that are the stock and trade of a lively design practice. For the final review, bring not just one project, but everything made over the course of this concerted research effort. The result may more closely resemble a science fair than a graphic design critique.

RGB: A color model for repre-senting visible light built up from three base colors: Red, Green, and Blue. It is an additive system where 100% Red plus 100% Green plus 100% Blue equals White. In additive color, each primary hue is added to the existing mix producing a lighter (brighter or higher value) color. Additive color is emitted; its material form is light, and its color is indexed to its frequency. Additive colors are native to screens. Combinations of Red, Green, and Blue light can produce a wide spectrum of color as continuous tone, photographic images.

CMYK: A color model for repre-senting the reflected light of inks, pigments, or dyes. It is a subtractive system, where 100% Cyan plus 100% Magenta plus 100% Yellow equals Black. Increasing the amount of any one of the base colors makes the resulting color darker. Subtractive color is reflected; it absorbs all frequencies of light that are not its color and reflects back only the frequencies that match. Subtractive colors are proper to paper. Combinations of Cyan, Magenta, and Yellow inks can be combined to produce a wide range of colors as continuous tone photographic images.

ABC, TV, NeXT

This is George Corrin [↓]. He practiced for 60 years as a set designer, a product designer, a graphic designer, and an exhibition designer. But he also almost didn't do any of those things.

Applying to Carnegie Institute of Technology in 1942, Corrin was brushed off with a curt note from the dean saying, "Negro students have not found the work of our department satisfactory to their needs," and suggested that he apply instead to Fisk University, a historically African American school in Nashville, Tennessee. Corrin replied with a cascade of recommendation letters and the school reversed its decision, admitting him as its first African American student. He graduated Phi Beta Kappa from what would become Carnegie Mellon University and went on to study set design at Yale University School of Drama, receiving an MFA in 1951. After a brief tour of military duty in the South Pacific, Corrin landed a design job at ABC Television in New York. He was fascinated by the technical and social possibilities of television and how design could participate. He soon had the chance to manifest his interest.

In 1960, the presidential debates were to be televised, for the first time, with ABC, CBS, and NBC collaborating on four broadcasts. ABC hosted the third debate, but due to a scheduling conflict, it would be staged remotely with Senator John F. Kennedy in an ABC studio in New York and Vice President Richard M. Nixon on a set in Los Angeles. This was a live broadcast where—using the electronic medium of television and cross-country data links—the two candidates would appear to be in the same room. The set design was central to pulling off this illusion. Corrin was tasked with creating two identical sets which would also look convincing as a split-screen image.

The design used a warm palette of gold fabric, wood-grained panels, and yellow paint. The fabric was ordered for both sets from the same mill, and likewise the panels from the same supplier. The paint was mixed in New York and then hand-carried on an airplane to Los Angeles to ensure an equivalent on-screen look. The lighting equipment in Los Angeles was replaced to precisely match New York and ABC coordinated with AT&T long-lines to reduce the coast-to-coast transmission lag.

The result was seamless [↑] [↓]; a mass electronic event watched by an astonishing 60 percent of US households with television sets—nearly 70 million people.

Corrin continued to work with ABC for 13 years on sets, on-screen graphics, and various design projects. In 1962, the network invited an American graphic designer with an already large reputation to create a new logo [↘].

The designer was Paul Rand [↓] and here is a portrait from at least a few years before.

Peretz Rosenbaum was born in Brooklyn in 1914. Painting signs for his father's grocery store led to studying design at Pratt Institute at night while attending public high school during the day for a more "practical" education. At Pratt, Rosenbaum assembled a portfolio of clean, modern design work and decided to modernize his name as well. Being Jewish, like being African American, at the time made working in design difficult. For all of its social rhetoric and its mostly liberal practitioners, the profession has a dreadful track record on diversity. Cloaking his Jewish identity, Rosenbaum took on the concise advertising-ready moniker made up from two sets of four letters: "Paul Rand."

Paul Rand is perhaps best known for his corporate identities, and the logomarks he designed thoroughly exploit Gestalt principles. For example, his ABC logo motivates the figure and ground relationship and the repetition of circular forms in the shapes of the letters and their negative spaces form a mark that sears itself into your eyes and brain. That one is still in use.

Also very well-known is his IBM logo [↑]. Rand worked with IBM for years on a variety of projects. He initially adjusted the existing logomark in 1956, modified it in 1960, and added its characteristic graphic stripes in 1972. Not every project was a success; he was commissioned by Ford Motor Company [↙] to redesign their mark, but it was never adopted. Others have lasted, like the logo for Westinghouse [↘].

The Westinghouse mark is built from a set of legible component parts, in specific relations to produce a coherent mark. So much so that it still says "Westinghouse" when it's split apart [↓].

This one's also a Paul Rand logo [↓].

By 1985, Paul Rand was living and working outside of New Haven, Connecticut. He was teaching at Yale University School of Art and was in great demand as a designer of corporate logos; these projects have large budgets and high stakes, and Rand knew it. When handling proposed new commissions, Rand would invite the potential commissioner to meet at the International House of Pancakes near his studio, have breakfast, and discuss their problem on neutral ground. Rand would then decide whether or not to accept the job. His baseline fee was $100,000.

The same year Steve Jobs founded NeXT Computer, Inc. after being fired from the company he founded, Apple Computer, by its board of directors. Jobs had a new idea that personal computers would go only so far, and he was interested in entering other markets with more powerful hardware. He wanted to make workstation computers, then priced out of reach of all but the largest organizations at $20–50,000. The NeXT machine cost only $6,500 for a base model and was marketed to universities, which would make the powerful computers and software applications accessible to students and faculty.

Jobs long admired Paul Rand's work and he invited Rand to work on this project. Rand agreed enthusiastically in this case—I don't even think a date at IHOP was required. He liked Jobs and the new machines were modern, black, austere; one was simply a cube. Jobs brought a team with him from Apple, including graphic designer Susan Kare. As before, Kare was responsible for the interface graphics in the new computer's operating system software.

When proposing a new logo, Rand typically produced a small printed booklet which collected his design research, exploration, and finally, a single recommendation. These were really proto-slide decks, and provide a clear look into the graphic design research and process, as well as a hopefully irrefutable argument to his clients for the proposed logo. The booklet provides a peek behind the curtain.

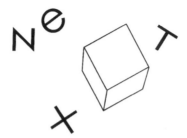

Rand's visit to NeXT Computer to present his logo proposal [↖] was, miraculously, captured on video. In the part I'd like to share the full staff is assembled to see what Rand's come up with. Here Rand is assisted by Kare as he pulls the booklets out of a box [↓].

Narrator: This morning at its offices in Silicon Valley, California, the company is about to get a first look at its new trademark, the signature it hopes to make familiar around the world. The designer Paul Rand created the logos for IBM, Westinghouse, UPS, and many others. Rand doesn't normally work for infant companies even if they could afford him. But NeXT isn't an ordinary startup.

Paul Rand: The idea—please don't open, don't look at the back first. This is the front. And don't get scared, this is not the design. I did this to sort of floor Steve when he saw it, you know and say, "Good Jesus, a hundred thousand bucks down the drain." ...

Steve Jobs: More important than building a product, we are in the process of architecting a company that will hopefully be much, much more incredible, the total will be much more incredible than the sum of its parts.

Now, even if he is invoking the rhetoric of Gestalt, I really don't want to let Steve Jobs have the last word, so I'm going to tack on a short addendum. I want to talk about Stewart Brand, another Bay Area character—a committed generalist who used his facility in design, writing, and publishing to make some unexpected connections. What follows is a significantly condensed biography and it takes the form of one (quite) long run-on sentence. This is an idea I've borrowed from Brand's own web page, which starts,

Let's see how many links I can cram in one fairly relevant sentence.

So, anyway, here we go.

Global Branding

High on his rooftop in North Beach, San Francisco, 1966, after ingesting a mild dose of LSD, Stewart Brand imagined the subtle curvature of the earth as he gazed out at the surrounding high-rises, noticing that they were not really parallel, the high-rises, and that the further you might view them from, the more extreme the curve, until finally, viewed from space, the Earth would resolve to a perfectly spherical marble, not dissimilar from the finite planet that Buckminster Fuller had been insisting we must all understand if we were ever to get civilization on this planet right, something Stewart Brand had been considering since his initial undergraduate coursework in biology at Stanford followed by his studies in design and photography at San Francisco Art Institute in 1962, which led him to spending three years on various Native American reservations in the American West culminating in a multimedia event in 1964 while simultaneously engaged by a growing interest in the space program at a time when the left was deeply suspicious of the defense industry initiative, so he tuned in, turned on, and dropped out, organizing The Trips Festival at The Longshoremen's Hall in San Francisco in 1966 before joining Ken Kesey's Band of Merry Pranksters traveling on a bus they named "Further" across the country which he professed to find mind opening and indirectly led to a profound conceptual leap, imagining a picture of the Earth from space and understanding its political aesthetic implications which inspired him to begin immediately the next morning making buttons that read,

Why haven't we seen a photograph of the whole earth yet?

and distributing these paranoiacally stated provocations widely, sending unsolicited packages to scientists, secretaries of state, astronauts, and thinkers like Marshall McLuhan and Buckminster Fuller (whose humbling response to "Why we haven't seen a photograph of the whole Earth?" was, "Well, you can only see about half the Earth at any given time"),

nonetheless, undeterred, these buttons [↑] and the wider campaign were picked up by newspapers, magazines, and the popular imagination, allegedly leading NASA to release full-color photographs of Earth [↙] from the Apollo missions of 1969

and by which time Brand had named and started work on the *Whole Earth Catalog*, whose second issue in the summer of 1969 featured the aforementioned photograph and whose subsequent covers also rigorously retained a photograph of the Earth from space, creating a remarkable series of covers [↙] [↓] [↘] formed by a repeated image and a specific cultural framework,

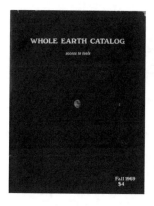  

and that Apollo 9 astronaut Rusty Schweickart, as head of the applications department of NASA, through persistent efforts, could not convince the scientific community at large that you couldn't see anything useful from space an idea directly at odds with the stated function and selection criteria of the *Whole Earth Catalog*, printed on the inside front cover, along with the reverse of the globe. It says,

> The *Whole Earth Catalog* functions as an evaluation and access device. With it, the user should know better what is worth getting and where and how to do the getting. An item is listed in the catalog if it is deemed useful as a tool, relevant to independent education, high quality or low cost, easily available by mail. Catalog listings are continually revised according to the experience and suggestions of catalog users and staff.

and meanwhile continuing his agenda to provide access to tools, the subtitled mission [↓] of the *Whole Earth Catalog*,

> *At the time, in fact, finances were not particularly on my mind. How To Make Money was not the design problem. (I'd heard and bought Ken Kesey's advice that you don't make money by making money: you have that in mind early on, but then you forget it and concentrate entirely on good product; the money comes to pass.) The problem was How to Generate a Low-Maintenance High-Yield Self-Sustaining Critical Information Service.*

Stewart Brand helped Doug Engelbart, computer scientist, design and organize what was later to be dubbed the "mother of all demos," or augmented human intellect, at the fall Joint Computer Conference in San Francisco at the Moscone Center, which introduced such occasionally useful and intimately familiar personal computing paradigms as the mouse [↘], linked text, windows, copying, pasting, and all the while

continuing to edit, publish, and direct the *Whole Earth Catalog* through several revisions, until 1972 with the publication of the *Last Whole Earth Catalog*, which was never intended to persist (only to get the word out there and adequately review the existing tools and resources for interested parties to use) [↓]

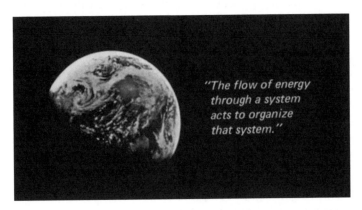

"The flow of energy through a system acts to organize that system."

with Scott Beach he organized the Demise Party to mark the end of the *Whole Earth Catalog* and engaged 1500 guests with $20,000 in cash that were the proceeds from four years of making and producing the catalog and providing access to tools for a mini-generation, so that by dawn the entire cash proceeds had been released to various parties, organizations, and individuals to do good with, a notion that Mr. Brand set out to explore himself following the precedent established by the Beatles on May 15th, 1968, when they formed Apple Corps to distribute funds to myriad artistic ventures and self-described as a kind of "Western communism" by founding the Point Foundation in 1972, and successfully giving away over $1,000,000 to assorted worthy individuals [↙] over the course of the next three years

while working on a 1972 article for *Rolling Stone* magazine, photographed by Annie Leibovitz, titled "Fanatic Life and Symbolic Death Among the Computer Bums," which detailed a then-fringe computer research and game playing being undertaken at Xerox PARC, the Stanford Artificial Intelligence Laboratory, and MIT, in which a Space War [↙] tournament was staged

with numerous bearded computer visionaries enjoying the visceral delights of free beer and computer games while exploring something else entirely—the useful exercise of thinking the world as a dynamically regulated and organic whole system, a topic that Brand investigated in his book published by Random House (established in 1925, when

Bennett Cerf and Donald Klopfer decided to publish "a few books on the side at random," including the first US edition of James Joyce's *Ulysses*) and which introduced fellow biologist Gregory Bateson into the ongoing discourse around self-organizing systems, feedback loops, and computer science through his book called *Two Cybernetic Frontiers*, which led, of course, to editing *Space Colonies* from 1976 and serving as an adviser to California Governor Edmund Brown from 1976 to 1979 while acquiescing finally to publish the *Next Whole Earth Catalog* in 1981, the peak edition, with a sizable advanced contract, powerful distribution, and encouraged Stewart to engage the problems, consequences, and opportunities at hand in the world of business which he did on the faculty of the Western Behavioral Institute of La Jolla, California, with a course he ran called Uncommon Courtesy School of Compassionate Skills, which gave courses in subjects like "Business as Service" and "Street Saint Skills," and whose instructions Brand continued to practice in subsequent publications insisting,

> It's our custom to print and try to explain our finances in each of our publications. Business we found does best when performed as a service. Service does best when it's approached as business.

and building on the Whole Earth legacy to its, some would say, inevitable evolution as a *The Whole Earth Software Catalog* [↓],

a review of the personal computer software which, becoming widely available and providing access to tools for a broad range of non-specialists who might soon find themselves tapping at their keyboards,

electronically chatting to each other in the pioneering online telecommu-
nications bulletin board system that Stewart Brand founded called
"The Well" (or Whole Earth 'Lectronic Link), often cited as a foundational
precedent for what became the World Wide Web, a global electronic
network originated in 1968 by the Advanced Research Projects Agency
of the United States Department of Defense to link scientists in San
Diego, Los Angeles, and Champaign-Urbana, Illinois, [↓]

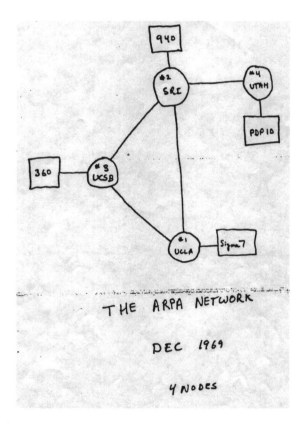

THE ARPA NETWORK

DEC 1969

4 NODES

which is showing no signs of slowing down, connecting uncountable
locations, real and imaginary, across the Earth today, and as the de facto
topic of a conference that Brand co-organized, co-founded with Kevin
Kelly, called "The Hackers Conference" televised since its creation in
1986 and organizing a loose knit group of software tinkerers, hardware
mechanics, and social engineers for exchange and disagreement; the
former Merry Prankster followed up as a visiting scientist at the Media
Lab at MIT in 1986 (later writing a book about his experience there) and
became a consultant with Royal Dutch Shell London, where he pio-
neered techniques of longterm scenario planning (which he developed

to a somewhat more concrete form in another project called "The Clock of the Long Now," a project with musician Brian Eno and supercomputer engineer Danny Hillis to design a very, very, very slow clock meant to last for 10,000 years and the point of which was to encourage good behavior, global responsibility, and social tendencies for the world's corporations, an idea that Brand extended by founding the Global Business Network to explore whole futures and extended scenarios for world economies based on the behaviors of its corporations and ending up back where this sentence started on the roof of Stewart Brand's North Beach apartment, tripping on LSD, trying to work out how he might think the world differently, if only we could see a photograph of the whole earth [↓].

We can't put it together. It is together.

Further Reading

Albers, Josef. *Interaction of Color*.
New Haven: Yale University Press, 1963.

Arnheim, Rudolf. *Visual Thinking*. Berkeley:
University of California Press, 1969.

Behrens, Roy R. "Art, Design and Gestalt
Theory." *Leonardo* 31, no. 4 (1998), 299.

Bill, Max, Pamela Johnston, and Karin
Gimmi. *Form, Function, Beauty = Gestalt*.
London: Architectural Association, 2010.

Brand, Stewart. *The Last Whole Earth
Catalog: Access to Tools*. Menlo Park, CA:
Portola Institute, 1971.

Dondis, Donis A. *A Primer of Visual
Literacy*. Cambridge, MA: MIT Press, 1973.

Ellis, Willis Davis, *A Source Book of
Gestalt Psychology*. New York: Harcourt,
Brace, 1938.

Gerstner, Karl. *Designing Programmes:
Four Essays and an Introduction*. London:
Tiranti, 1964.

Kepes, György. *Language of Vision*.
Chicago: P. Theobald, 1967.

Lange, Alexandra. "The Woman Who Gave
the Macintosh a Smile," *The New Yorker*,
April 19, 2018.

Lupton, Ellen, and J. Abbott Miller.
"Language of Vision," in *Design Writing
Research*. New York: Kiosk, 1996.

Munari, Bruno. *Bruno Munari: The Triangle*.
Mantova: Corraini, 2007.

Rand, Paul. *Design, Form and Chaos*.
New Haven: Yale University Press, 1993.

Reinfurt, David, and Robert Wiesenberger.
Muriel Cooper. Cambridge, MA: MIT Press,
2017.

"Susan Kare, Iconographer," EG
Conference video, 19:38, May, 2014,
https://vimeo.com/97583369

Tanchis, Aldo, and Bruno Munari. *Bruno
Munari: Design As Art*. Cambridge, MA:
MIT Press, 1987.

Wertheimer, Max, Lothar Spillmann, and
Michael Wertheimer. *On Perceived Motion
and Figural Organization*. Cambridge, MA:
MIT Press, 2012.

http://www.g-e-s-t-a-l-t.org

I-N-T-E-R-F-A-C-E

Dial +44 20 3598 2801, and you'll hear this:

> **Phone:** At the third stroke it will be 6:20 and 40 seconds. [Three beeps]
> At the third stroke it will be 6:20 and 50 seconds. [Three beeps]
> At the third stroke it will be 6:21 precisely. [Three beeps]

It's a "speaking clock," an automated electronic announcement which provides the current time. The distinctive voice belongs to Pat Simmons, a former London Telephone Exchange employee who spoke the time from 1963 until 1985. Simmons followed Jane Cain [↓], the "golden voice" of the first British telephone time system starting in 1936.

That first set up was a room-sized electric mechanism which produced an automated announcement from glass disk recordings of spoken audio bits. Here is Pat Simmons [↓] recording numbers and sentence fragments.

Dialing "T-I-M" from any UK telephone at the time set this elaborate machine running. Before this, speaking clocks were delivered live by an

operator sitting in front of a clock face, answering phone calls, and reading out the time [↓].

Of course what you hear live when you call the number above depends
on exactly when you call. The voice, well that's not so live. Simmons
spoke the clock only from 1963 until 1985 and this service is a software
simulation run by enthusiasts at telephonesuk.co.uk. Live, recorded, or
programmed, a speaking clock is clearly an anachronism. But, it also provides a crisp model for thinking around something quite contemporary:
the interface.

> **Jane Cain:** At the third stroke it will be 8:57 precisely.

> **Pat Simmons:** At the third stroke it will be 7:02 and forty-seconds.

> **Man's voice:** At the third stroke the time sponsored by Accurist will be
> 10:52 and 10 seconds.

Each has a particular quality and it's easy enough to imagine those
voices as the personality, or even the design, of this interface. Call the
speaking clock and you're interacting with a front end, a "user experience"—you're given a simple friendly face for a complex process which
remains hidden.

> Whatever lies between is called interface. Whatever allows us to link to
> different elements, to reconcile them, to put them into communication.

That definition was offered in 1987 by Italian critic Giancarlo Barbacetto
in his introduction to *Design Interface*. The book chronicled the Olivetti
Typewriter Corporation's early attempts at designing user controls for

photocopiers, computers, typewriters, and calculators. Barbacetto places this design task in a broad cultural and temporal context. Appearing opposite his introduction is a reproduction of the Rosetta Stone, offered up as a kind of original, ur-interface—a shared surface which facilitates communication between otherwise irreconcilable languages and cultures. The Rosetta Stone [↙] records three different languages all relaying the same message. The recovery of this "shared surface" in 1799 allowed the deciphering of Egyptian hieroglyphs.

Barbacetto continues from the Rosetta Stone to an impossibly broad scoping of the concept of interface and lands on this, a public clocktower in the Piazza San Marco in Venice [↗]. It's the first public clock and it's set at the center of a merchant city, where shared time would have significant consequences for shipping and commerce. He goes on,

> An extremely powerful and everyday filter is the clock. The first machine made available to all from high atop a tower ready to interface humans and time. The clock tore humans away from lived time marked by natural rhythms and by the duties of seasonal social labor and delivered into the power of measured time, objective and abstract. The work time of urban merchants, the interest time of the money lender, the factory time of industry. First the bells of the city clocktower, later the mill siren, erased cyclical time that moved, the rhythm of the seasonal return, of a certain kind of game, the ripening of a plant, the dependable rising of the sun. Cyclical

time was a great exorcism of death—the moon that returns is the first dead man returning, repetition is the life of the world, history is nothing but the reiteration of a single original event; time is Kronos, the great primordial judge.

After the arrival of the clock all that became a memory and a myth. Time became linear, homogenous, empty, irreversible, cumulative, oriented towards a goal. Even modern mechanical thought prefers rectilinear motion to circular motion. Clocks mark the separation between work time (the value time of production), and free time, but today even the physicality of the chimes of the clocktower is obscured by the digital information time, the absolute acceleration of the discontinuity in the contemporaneity of computer time.

Olivetti's first large computer (built in 1959) was named the Elea, after the colony in Magna Graecia where, in the fifth century B.C. the school of philosophy of Parmenides and Zeno was born. "Elea computer"—the name itself is like saying mathematical rationality and philosophical discourse, algorithm and hermeneutics.

("Algorithm and hermeneutics" or in other words, a definite pattern and how things get their meanings.)

It is this impossible synthesis that communicative signs seek to attain. Extreme formalization of the message and infinite production of meaning;

(Something highly regular, repeated with a kind of infinite production of meaning within—think of the alphabet, for example.)

That clock in Piazza San Marco has several different displays of the time. The central display is a round clock face which shows the months, or the time of the astronomical zodiac throughout the year, as well as the minutes. The next layer up shows the Roman numeral "XI," and the Arabic numerals "5" and "5." So, it's currently 11:55 am. These are large blue tiles, and it looks like a digital clock and these flip every 15 minutes using a large wheel mechanism inside. Throughout this clock there's play with how the time is represented and displayed, geared toward a pluralistic, cosmopolitan time as Venice was a trading place for myriad cultures.

How the zodiac is represented, the distinction between Roman numerals and Arabic digits, the relative scale of the clock hands are each interface design decisions.

Here's a closer view [↓].

An interface is inevitably a product of its culture. It's made in a specific time and place to be used in a specific time and place, and design decisions reflect shared conventions, assumptions, and histories from that setting. An interface now would not necessarily work 20 years in the future.

"Well, of course," you say. But it is not only technical considerations, but cultural ones that might be an interface's Achilles' heel. Imagine trying to explain the iPhone messages interface [↙] [↘] to someone in 1971, or in 2004 for that matter.

It's simple enough, but the nuance of how it can be used would be lost in the cultural distance. Thirty years in the future, it may be similarly illegible.

"Interface" is an extraordinarily elastic word. Definitions from fields as diverse as chemistry, theater, fashion, and computer science describe interface as "a shared boundary," "a contact surface," "a border condition," and "a process or active threshold." All of these definitions share a central tenet—an interface is a thing itself. Its design decisions change not only what it looks like, but also how it works. And these interfaces have the possibility of conveying more than simply utility, they may also transmit a point of view.

Interfaces surround us, manifested in compiled code, running on silicon chips, and fronting the computer services we all use, all the time. So, we had better understand at least a little about how they are made.

The June 15, 2015 issue of *Bloomberg Businessweek* was given over to a single text by writer and computer programmer Paul Ford. "Code: An Essay" presents fundamentals of programming languages and techniques for a broad audience, with depth and finesse. In its introduction, Ford offers a concise and surprisingly robust definition of a computer:

> A computer is a clock with benefits.

and continues ...

> They all work the same, doing second-grade math, one step at a time: Tick, take a number and put it in box one. Tick, take another number, put it in box two. Tick, operate (an operation might be addition or subtraction) on those two numbers and put the resulting number in box one. Tick, check if the result is zero, and if it is, go to some other box and follow a new set of instructions. A computer's processing power is even measured by the rate of its CPU, called "clock speed."

If your computer is (already) fundamentally a clock, then clearly the telephone service you dialed at the beginning of this essay is more of an antique curiosity than a working tool. Even a regular wristwatch seems like a genteel affordance when your phone, your laptop, and every message you send through these already registers the time. And in the face of all this, the Apple Watch has arrived. Is it some kind of cutting edge anachronism?

Well, it does have an extremely challenging interface-design problem. Its touchscreen is tiny [↑], screen real estate is limited, batteries are finite, and fingers are not shrinking any time soon. The ways in which Watch OS software solves many of these interface design issues is instructive. The device's screen lights only when you raise your wrist to look at it. The watch's face can be almost instantly swapped out with a strong push and a swipe. The watch reveals its full range of utilities when you press the "digital crown" and this pulls up the Launcher, a kind of iOS home screen seen through a roving digital magnifying lens. From here, the watch fluidly transforms itself into an iPod, mail reader, weather station, text messager, and so on. What is interesting is not so much what the watch can do, but rather how what it can do is all packaged behind its familiar clock interface.

Amid the hyperbole of the official Apple Watch design video in which he introduces the product, Jonathan Ive describes the interface.

> **Jonathan Ive:** The watch senses that you're raising your wrist, and then activates the display. You see, an organization of apps that, while new, is somehow familiar. Navigation is fluid and vital. Magnifying content on a small display is fundamentally important. So we've developed a whole new interface specific to the challenges associated with a product this small.
>
> The digital crown is a remarkable input device. It fluidly zooms into apps. It enables nimble, precise adjustments and, critically, you can use it without obstructing the display. It's also the home button. Apps designed for light-weight interaction. Smart replies and dictation let you respond quickly to messages. Glances let you swipe through information efficiently....

* * *

Standing more or less alone on a train platform in the small Swiss town of St. Margarethen one morning around 6:00 am, I noticed two station clocks in my line of sight. They were the iconic Swiss Railway clocks designed by Hans Hilfiker in 1944. It's a graphically concise clock face with no numbers, only bold black strokes marking hours, smaller (still bold) strokes for minutes, and two workman-like arms for the hours and minutes. Seconds, however, are registered by a bright red lollipop of a hand [↘].

Its distinctive form was added in 1953 and based on the shape of an engineer's signalling disk used to indicate when a train is clear to depart the station. The resulting clock face design is austere, specific, and exaggeratedly functional [↙].

It is so particular that Apple even "borrowed" [↗] it for the clock app on iPad before being sued by Swiss Federal Railways and eventually settling on a $22.4M licensing fee. (The offending interface was removed in iOS 7.)

Staring at the two clocks through my morning fog, I noticed that they were perfectly synchronized. I suppose, this shouldn't be surprising, particularly in a train station (and a Swiss train station at that), where inaccurate clocks would have definite consequences on how passengers get where they are going. But as I stood staring at the clock close to me and the one across the tracks on another platform, I noticed something surprising. Each time the second hands reached the top, they paused in a decidedly long click, after which, the two continued again to sweep around the face. These clocks, linked and synchronized by radio signals, implement an accurate and consistent clock system. You can be sure standing on a rural train platform in St. Margarethen or in the central station in Zürich that the clock you are looking at tells the same time, and the engineer driving the train which connects the two also reads the same time.

But what the clock looks like is essential for this to work. Hilfiker's clock face design is typically "Swiss," with minimal articulation, extreme contrast, and clearly rendered functional distinctions that suggest precision, efficiency, simplicity. The bright red second hand can be seen from a distance so you can easily scan that these clocks are in sync. Even the once-a-minute pause, while functional, also communicates accuracy.

As I stood looking at Hilfiker's clock that morning [↑] (the blank stare of its graphics looking back), I was using a carefully orchestrated interface— an interface between me and the train yet to arrive, coordinating our communication and assuring me that if I trust it, I'll get where I'm going. In the end, I did.

Assignment 1, Apple Watch

Redesign the face of Apple Watch in order to change the way time is read.

This is an in-depth, semester-length assignment.

Weeks 1–2: Begin by reading widely about a variety of means for time-keeping. From this basis, identify one aspect of time-keeping and display of particular interest. This could be an investigation of sundials or sand clocks; it could be a look into the changing schedules of contemporary workers; circadian rhythms and sleep cycles; or how an atomic clock keeps time. What is chosen must sustain work over the semester, so it should be genuinely fascinating.

Weeks 3–4: Prepare a brief research presentation on the area of interest. This presentation (more of a performance) must be exactly 16 minutes long. The presentation cannot run shorter. If it runs long, it will be cut off. Consider including some kind of temporal flexibility into the presentation.

Weeks 5–11: Begin sketching the clock interface, and work iteratively every week to develop the concept both conceptually and visually. Along with each week of development, review all work as a group. This is an extended process by design so that an idea can emerge from careful working and reworking of an initial idea which addresses a fundamental interest.

Week 12: Prepare a five to eight minute video that demonstrates the proposed clock interface, how it works, what it looks like, how it behaves, and why it matters.

On September 10, 2014, CEO Tim Cook stood on stage at an Apple Computer special event announcing he had "one more thing" to show the audience of developers, reporters, and fans. The one more thing was Apple Watch, a hotly anticipated hardware which took the outer form of a standard wristwatch but whose functional relationship to a wristwatch was that of the iPhone to a rotary-dial hard-wired Bell telephone. The Apple Watch is of both the future and the past, impossibly retrograde and fantastically forward-pointing. Apple Watch can send email, transcribe and send text messages, show the next events on a calendar, navigate step-by-step to a destination, forecast the weather, keep track of daily exercise, measure and record heartbeats, play podcasts, Apple Pay for goods and services, and so on. Many of its functions were familiar from the iPhone, but the way in which these were now presented to the user was entirely novel. For example, Calendar was reconceived from the spatial metaphor of a month at time, days organized on a two-dimensional grid to a temporal sequence of notifications delivered over the course of a day. Messages was also redesigned from a digressive, interactive chat tool to a more immediate and lower bandwidth channel to encourage brief replies with templated responses such as "Hello!" "What's up?" and "On my way." These changes, accommodations to the small screen size and bodily location, were interface design changes. The interface is a collection of choices and together these form a specific point of view which has consequences on how the watch is used.

Using the existing Apple Watch Human Interface guidelines and departing from the conventions only if and when necessary should help projects be more comparable from one student to another, as well as more plausible within the existing Apple Watch interface. As it turns out, redesign of the Apple Watch clock face is the one part of the interface which Apple has identified as off-limits to third-party developers.

Zapotecs & Pulsars

Monte Albán is a pre-Columbian site above Oaxaca, in central Mexico which I visited in 2015 with my parents-in-law, who had been there several times before. I was struck by the overlap of past and present at the site, where an ancient Zapotec city and its foundations overlook the modern city of Oaxaca.

One afternoon, my father-in-law led us up the back way toward Monte Albán. As you crest a small hill, this [↓] is what you see—just an expanse. The scale is a bit hard to take in at first. It's gigantic.

It has a regular orthogonal layout of pyramid structures, inset with cere-monial grounds entered by the steps on the right. It was a ritual site, a sacred site, where (almost) nobody lived. Zapotec culture was particu-larly active in the central valleys of southern Mexico from about 700 B.C. to 700 A.D., and while it was not as large or long as some other native Mexican cultures, its language has persisted and is still spoken. The primitive forms and its distinct ceremonial layout makes it easy to cast yourself back in time. Monte Albán was a site for events that marked specific moments in time. It's kind of a walk-in clock.

We spent the day climbing up and down the various pyramids, examining the place. There was a ball court, where a ritual game was played. There were locations for sacrifices, for celebrations, births, funerals, and so on.

All the buildings are rectangular except for this [↓] structure at the center. It's also the only building that is meant to be entered. It was the astronomical observatory and used only by Zapotec astronomers (who were also, in a reason-meets-faith synchrony, Zapotec priests). Members of this sect would enter, look up, read the stars or the sun in the sky, and then emerge to announce what time it was. Time-keeping was a divine act for Zapotecs, received by astronomer-priests directly from the heavens.

The site is also heavily populated with writing that marks ceremonial sites and events, recording dates from 700 B.C. using the oldest known example of a Mesoamerican calendar. Inscribed in stone, either directly on buildings or on free-standing upright slabs (stela), the writing system is thought to combine logographic, ideographic, pictographic, even alphabetic glyphs. This is not unique, but the combination of all of these systems in one culture is rare.

LOGOGRAPHIC: A writing system where glyphs stand for words or meaningful components of words (morphemes) in a language. No writing system can be entirely logographic, but must include some phonetic element, either as part the logogram or as its own glyph.

IDEOGRAPHIC: A writing system where glyphs stand for ideas or concepts, not specific words in a language. In this system, there is no one-to-one link between symbol and language, therefore there is also no single way to read these glyphs. No writing system can be entirely ideographic and maintain the full expressive capacity of a language.

PICTOGRAPHIC: A writing system where glyphs resemble the objects that they stand for. In this system, there is no one—to—one link between symbol and language, therefore there is also no single way to read these glyphs. No writing system can be entirely pictographic and maintain the full expressive capacity of a language.

ALPHABETIC: A writing system where glyphs stand for sounds in a spoken language. In this system, there is a one—to—one link between symbol and language, where definite order—ings of the glyphs (spelling) combine to form specific words in a language.

Inscriptions at Monte Albán are catalogued and numbered. Here are two I saw when I was there—stela 12 [↙] and stela 13 [↘]. These contain the oldest recorded dates in pre-Columbian Mexico.

Dates are recorded as combinations of symbol glyphs and numerical tally marks. The inscriptions are read from top to bottom. For example, the stone on the left marks a year with an abstract symbol which sits on a fig- urative glyph combined with four dots. The composite symbol identifies a specific day in the calendar.

The Zapotec calendar works like other Mesoamerican calendars, using both a sacred cycle of 260 days as well as a solar cycle of 365 days.

As both cycles were used at once, then any one day within a longer period was uniquely identified using a combination of a day in the solar calendar and a day in the sacred calendar to make one composite and unique date.

A similarly circular logic was applied to the sacred calendar itself. Each of its 20 days are marked by a symbol which was combined in permutation with a number from 1–13. Unique combinations in series of each digit (13) together with each symbol (20) produced a period of ($13 \times 20 = 260$) discrete dates. (The solar calendar was also segregated, marking its 365 days into four equal periods to produce its dates.)

It's easiest to understand the mechanics of the Zapotec calendar by imagining two wheels of different sizes placed side by side.

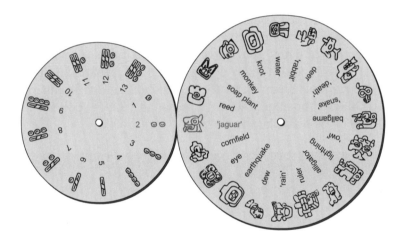

As you spin one wheel, the other also spins. They are different sizes (like gears) and the speed at which either wheel turns is a function of its radius. So, for example, in the sacred calendar above, the smaller wheel shows the days [↖] represented by 13 digits. (These digits are really a visual tally system where dots are one and lines are five.) The larger wheel [↗] is a collection of glyphs which are pictograms for the sacred symbols including "rabbit," "water," or "monkey." As the two wheels move (ie., time moves forward) then a "date" is produced which is a composite of the two wheels, marked by a unique combination of digit and symbol. So, for example, today might be "three owl," "four ball-game," or "five snake."

Finally, since the two calendars (sacred and solar) were of different lengths, they would correlate after a period of time. In this case, the sacred calendar's 260 days and the solar calendar's 365 synchronize every 18,980 days, or 52 years. (5 × 52 = 260 and 5 × 73 = 365, and they share a common denominator, then 5 × 52 × 73 = 18,980.)

Fifty-two years was also the upper limit of reasonable Zapotec life expectancy. At the end of the cycle, an astronomer-priest would enter the observatory at Monte Albán, check the location of the constellation Pleiades, and, if it was in the correct place in the sky then the gods were happy. And if the gods were happy then the cycle begins again, since stars move in regular and predictable patterns. Zapotecs did not mark the passing of these longer chunks of time. So at the end of 52 years it's time for the next calendar—the beginning of time, once again.

* * *

This second part is about pulsars. A pulsar is a rotating neutron star which emits light at a (very) regular radio frequency. A neutron star is the collapsed core of a "giant" star, formed by a supernova explosion. It is extremely small and extremely dense. When the pulsar spins, light is emitted as a periodic beam on a very regular cycle, much like an inter-stellar lighthouse. You might think of a pulsar as a kind of cosmic clock, ticking away in the distant universe [↓].

I want to look at a couple artworks that might shed some light. This sculpture is by Naum Gabo from 1919 [↓]. He called it a kinetic construction, and it's composed of a long piece of metal connected to a hidden motor in its base that, when put into motion, looks like a solid object. When moving, the thin aluminum strip conjures a pulsing, sinuous, three-dimensional form. Like a pulsar, and like a clock even, its motion is periodic and regular. What I like in this work is the way it makes me think about the third dimension as dependent on movement, or any solid shape as a function of time. The work is called *Standing Wave*.

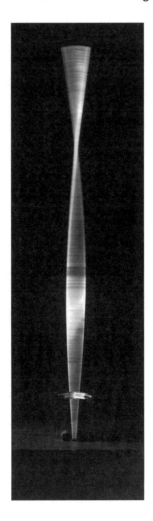

The second artwork is a photograph by Hiroshi Sugimoto. It is from a series called *Theatres* in which he set up his camera in a cinema and left the lens open for the full running time of a film. This picture was made south of San Francisco in 1993. Sugimoto describes that "to watch a two-hour movie is simply to look at 172,800 photographic afterimages." So what you see in his image is every photograph in the film passing by at 24 frames per second and collapsed into one composite white rectangle [↓]. This still picture contains the entire two hours, and if only you could change the speed of your eyes, you might even be able watch it. The camera also records the traces of everything else that happens in the meantime—in this case, planes taking off from and landing at San Francisco International Airport.

What these two artworks have in common they also share with the pulsar star: a regular, periodic movement produces their form.

The first electronic digital wristwatch was manufactured by Hamilton watch company of Lancaster, Pennsylvania, in 1972. Before this, watches were analog with hour and minute hands rotating on a 12-hour dial. Analog watches were quick and convenient—at a glance you could quickly see what time it is by the relative configuration of the hands on the face. A digital watch was necessarily slower. The time spells out as a sequence of digits, set to either 12- or 24-hour time.

An analog wristwatch "tells" or measures the time, but here on the Pulsar's electronic digit-based display, you have to "read" the time. And you even had to press a button to turn on the display. When you do, the current time reads not as an approximate value but as a definite set of futuristic glowing red numbers. The watch in some ways may have been a step back in everyday use, but its visual rhetoric stakes a claim to precision. It certainly looks more accurate [↓].

I think it is useful to try to understand how this looked when it appeared, so I want to now share a video from 1972 that Hamilton made to introduce the Pulsar.

Narrator: Time, the endless river transporting some, engulfing others. A stream upon which information explodes, communications multiply, technology accelerates into ever new life. Yet the flow of time is constant. Sixty-seconds every minute. Sixty minutes every hour. Twenty-four hours every day. How then can we even keep up to do more, be more, live more completely within the same non-expandable framework of time? Perhaps one answer: find better ways to track and use the time we have to better take our own measure. To better make use of ourselves. But if time is the measure of man, what might be the ultimate measure of time itself?

An American Revolution. The place, Lancaster, Pennsylvania. The time, now. The goal, to find and use the most advanced technology on Earth to create the most accurate, most rugged, most reliable, easiest to use wrist timepiece anyone can own. Begin with the beat of time itself. The oscillation of a quartz crystal. 32,768 times a second. A frequency that will be controlled to guarantee an accuracy within 60 seconds a year. But each quartz crystal is unique. Its frequency differing slightly from every other crystal. How then achieve the accuracy required? First, each crystal is deliberately aged, put into life cycle for two weeks to stabilize. Then, its actual frequency is measured, and the direction and degree of desired performance noted. Meanwhile, laser beams are cutting apart the resistance network that will be used to regulate each crystal. Each one, a network of fifty tantalum nitrate resistors, the most stable resistance material known. Each network evaporated onto a ceramic substrate, one of the few materials able to withstand the heat of vaporization and connected with gold conductors. Subsequently two trimmer condensers are added, so that each Pulsar can be adjusted at the factory and by the local jeweler to fulfill over its entire life the extraordinary accuracy guaranteed to its owner. But how can the oscillations of a quartz crystal be transformed into the exact date, day of the month, hour, minute, second?

The need? A computer, highly sophisticated, multi-functional, yet small enough to easily fit on your wrist. The solution: a logic chip so small its production and testing can be viewed satisfactorily only under a microscope yet containing the equivalent of more than 1,500 solid state devices. A logic chip that can compute and store the exact time and date. That can divide the frequency of the quartz crystal into the number of impulses actually needed. The electrical properties of each logic chip are carefully measured so that each chip can be precisely mated to the one quartz crystal that will ensure optimum performance. The pulses of electrical energy are now ready to activate a readable display.

What is the best possible way to display the time? Without ambiguity, without noise. Direct reading numbers that clearly, unmistakably communicate the time with the precision that matches the accuracy of Pulsar.

* * *

I have a postscript. Recently in New York City, there was a "super blue moon." I saw it from my balcony. That moon was "super" because it was close to the Earth in its orbit, so it looked bigger, and it was "blue" because it was the second full moon in the same month. Those two cycles combined to make this relatively rare phenomenon of the super blue moon. Seeing this reminded me how many things already work like those Zapotec calendars. This time, the super blue moon was widely announced by the astronomer-priests of contemporary news media.

* * *

A second postscript—when I was up on Monte Albán and looking around, we were using a popular guidebook [↓]. My father-in-law and my daughter were sharing the book, and somehow in a scramble up a pyramid or otherwise, the book was misplaced. We looked and asked around, but never found it.

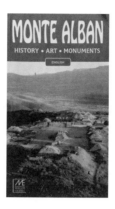

The next day my wife was thumbing through a second copy of the guidebook when she noticed in the fuzzy detail of one of the photos an unmistakeable pair of distinctive silhouettes. She zoomed in on the printed image with her phone's camera, and yes, it was true. She showed the picture to her sister. Both agreed: "Yes, that's our mother and father at Monte Albán." They wore the right clothes, it would have been the right time, and although we couldn't see faces, there was no mistaking it. So here was my father-in-law, an image from the past, printed in the guidebook from the place he just was [↓], in the guidebook he'd just lost at that place. Amazing. Cosmic, even.

Olivetti's Interfaces

Camillo Olivetti [↗] was born toward the end of the 19th century in Ivrea, in the northwest of Italy. He studied to be an engineer in Turin and left for what we now call Silicon Valley on a fellowship to Stanford University in the electrical engineering department. While there, Olivetti came across a new American invention he had not seen before: the Underwood mechanical typewriter. Olivetti was intrigued. He returned to Ivrea after completing the fellowship and joined up with a couple of childhood friends to set up a new company called Centimetro, Grammo, Secondo to manufacture precision instruments for measuring distance, mass, and time. This was a moment when manufacturing was ramping up in the industrial corridors of northern Italy, so precise devices to measure calibrations of finer and smaller degrees were in demand. It was also important to Olivetti to do this both with his childhood friends and in his hometown—he felt instinctively that a business has a direct responsibil-ity to the context in which it operates. If successful, the company would provide jobs and prosperity to Ivrea. However, it wasn't.

And so he returned to California for another stint at Stanford. This time he looked into the typewriter more closely, managed to make contact with people working on the machine, and returned to Italy with a complete set of blueprints. Olivetti set up another new company, the Olivetti Typewriter Corporation, which would design and manufacture the machines. Related to his thoughts on the responsibilities of a company to its context, he also believed it was important to understand typewriters within the *cultural context of writing,* the way that writing affects society and conversely, the way in which society shapes writing. Writing mechanistically changes things: you no longer use your own hand, one letter might look like another, the machine might even make writing more like factory work. So, although he had the blueprints for the machine, being an engineer Camillo redesigned it from the ground up. The Olivetti typewriter [↙] was a completely different type of writing machine, one whose design aimed to make writing with it more individual, more pleasurable, more human.

The Olivetti company became pretty successful pretty quickly and built a larger factory. Alongside the idea that its typewriters might make writing by machine more human, Olivetti also thought that the company must do something positive for its workers—provide jobs, produce an economic base for his hometown. Famously, the new Olivetti factory building was designed with large windows that face the Italian Alps so that the workers might look at the mountains as they assembled typewriters. Olivetti debuted the typewriter at the Turin International—a kind of World's Fair dedicated to labor and industry—in 1911, where they showed not only the typewriters but all of the tooling and process plus biographies of the factory workers. It was, and remains, a distinct approach, a convincing approach.

Olivetti was soon a family business. Camillo's son Adriano Olivetti started working in the company from 1929 and eventually he ran it. Adriano had an even more committed point of view about the relationship of this company to the society it worked in. But he saw a fundamental problem with making typewriters and making writing machines, which he described simply that machines and humans are hostile to each other; it's (essentially) dehumanizing to use a machine. Using a machine too long or too mindlessly, a person might start to adopt the logic and mindset of a machine. He also insisted that design should be elevated within the company and that it should run through all aspects and through all scales of the organization. He had a firm belief that better design leads to a better society; that design itself is a good, a net positive.

So, if the typewriter was a commercial good, then design was a social good: something the company could amplify and distribute throughout society. This approach is explicitly not about creating desire through design. Rather, this is about creating things which will enrich society rather than feed off of it.

Olivetti considered design central to the mission of the company. Design, he argued, was a medium for reconciling work and life, technology and people. Design could broker our relationships with machines, and the careful consideration of design would let us work with the speed and convenience of increasingly automated machines while not losing our essential humanity. Design could be a medium for mitigating this complex and fraught interface.

Olivetti did this a few ways. One was through an ambitious design commissioning program, hiring contemporary artists to do design work. For example, sculptor Marcello Nizzoli was commissioned to design an adding machine, the Divisumma 24 [↙] [↘]. Nizzoli was brought in to give that product a form, and he did give it a rather sculptural, even personal, form, but he also solved the problem with a form that corresponds directly to the mechanism within it.

Adriano Olivetti believed that by hiring an artist who has a distinct point of view—that's what they're communicating with society at large through their work—it would give people new ways to think about the world and circulate some alternative narratives other than the ones being put forth by more ruthlessly commercial enterprises. Olivetti believed that having an artist work as a designer on products manufactured in multiple and distributed widely would provide an effective vehicle for injecting the unique point of view of artists into society at a powerful scale.

Another product Nizzoli designed was the Lettera 22 typewriter [↙]. This small portable machine was a big hit for Olivetti.

Almost all of the keys on its interface are round and black. The corresponding letter or number is in the center of the circle. It is clearly recognizable as a typewriter keyboard. But one key is bright red and has no identifying type on it. What key is that? Well, it is the carriage return. That key has a different function; instead of typing some character, this key returns the typewriter mechanism to the beginning of a new line. It has a different function and therefore a different color. But also, this one red key gives the product a bit of personality. It feels human and particular. Olivetti liked to describe design as the cultural dividend of a product. A product existed, people used it, but then there is a little something extra, maybe joy or surprise or pleasure, and this extra is a gift, returned to the society in which the product works. This one red key is design's dividend.

By 1955, Olivetti realized that computers were on the horizon and the business would move from typewriters and adding machines to calculators and computers. Adriano Olivetti's son Roberto together with a brilliant engineer, Mario Tchou, were put in charge [↓].

Olivetti Electronics was established as a separate division and operated from a corporate research center in Connecticut, near the headquarters of the leading computer manufacturer of the time, IBM. Olivetti Electronics had fantastic success rather quickly. Within two years the first Olivetti computer arrived, the Macchina Zero. A few years later, Olivetti released its second computer, the Elea 9000.

For that computer, Olivetti brought in a designer to work on not just the body, the architecture of the machine itself—remember these are room-size computers at the time—but also, and importantly, to design the machine's human interface. Ettore Sottsass was charged with these tasks. Here you see the interface [↗]. You can see, the computer is the room [↖], but the interface is a seam that joins the human and the large, unknowably complex machinery. This is exactly the moment when Olivetti thought design could bring a real value back to society—mitigating, easing, facilitating, and making working with a machine a bit more human.

The Elea 9000 was relatively successful, and the electronics division continued. Pier Giorgio Perotto was working as an engineer for Olivetti Electronics and he had the new idea that there might be something much, much smaller than a room-sized computer. The new "personal" computer he imagined would be more like an amplified adding machine. This would be the Olivetti Programma 101 [↓], identified by Steve Jobs as the first desktop computer.

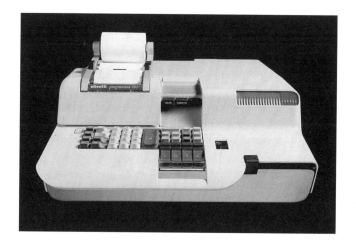

The Programma 101 was an electronic calculator with additional logic within that allowed it to run computer programs. You could instruct the 101 to do a certain set of calculations in a certain order and include logic that says, if it adds up to this, then do this, or if it doesn't add up then do something else. All of this was embedded in this one small machine. And it was a giant hit when it first appeared at the 1964 World's Fair in New York. The machine was both a media and commercial success almost immediately. This computer lived on a desk or table, and you could do things like perform statistical analysis, or auto-tabulate data by writing and running a computer program. This was quickly useful for businesses, universities, and even hobbyists. The Programma 101 included simple instructions for its reduced programming language which was pretty easy to learn. But what it introduced more consequentially was the idea of computer programming, a kind of definite logic, a script, a particular set of instructions that could behave autonomously of the user given the proper codes and starting conditions. This first personal computer looks mostly like a robust adding machine and that was intentional.

In 1960, several years before the Programma 101 was released, Roberto Olivetti died unexpectedly and co-director of Olivetti Electronics, Mario Tchou, was killed in an auto accident. At the same time, Olivetti Electronics started losing money and rather than subject itself to grave financial losses, the company decided to sell off its electronics unit—personnel intact—to General Electric. Perotto, the engineer working on Programma 101 realized this could be the end of his project. He internally reclassified the product as an adding machine and the project remained within the Olivetti division. He installed his team in an off-site garage so that no one would see what they were doing, and they continued to work.

The Programma 101 was designed by Mario Bellini, an Italian architect, who at the same time was also designing prototypes for Autogrill (a fast food chain found along Italian highways), designing buildings, exhibitions, and graphics. Bellini's approach was to make this "computer" speak the formal language of an adding machine. The numeric keyboard is prominent, an output paper tape provides display, and the unit is compact enough for one person to use on a desktop. It was perhaps a sleeker, more modern or even futuristic adding machine, but still clearly fit within that product category. This was meant to be read as an electronic calculator.

There was a second motivation for Perotto's reclassification of the Programma 101—to make the product more palatable, more understandable to people who had no idea what a "personal computer" might be. So rather than try to sell the public on a personal computer, they tried to sell an adding machine that also remembers things and can process instructions.

You might think about the Apple Watch in a similar way. It's really not a watch, is it? Telling time is not what it's doing. Rather, the watch uses the familiar "social furniture" of a watch. You know how to wear a watch. You know what to do with a watch. But you don't write e-mails on your watch, well at least not until now.

* * *

I want to talk about a book, *Design Interface*, edited by Gianni Barbacetto and published in 1987 in more detail. The book [↗] chronicles one concise project by two designers who worked collaboratively for forty years, Perry King and Santiago Miranda.

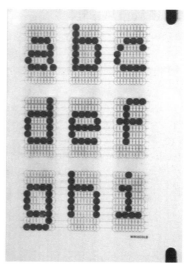

King and Miranda worked with Olivetti on a number of different projects, including some of the first LED-based signage and a typeface to render letters on electronic displays [↗] in the most legible but also most human way. So, for example, you can see how the "g" is curved. It doesn't look like a machine, there's a bit of humanity in the equation.

In 1984, Olivetti was expanding its product range to include photocopiers and fax machines. These were relatively new as broad consumer items and were increasingly powerful and also complex. New interfaces were needed beyond the small collection of existing buttons and switches and these buttons and switches were soon transitioning to flat-membrane electronic layouts that merged display and control. King and Miranda were asked to design an interface language for these new machines, and decided to attack the problem with a significant research effort.

They imagined more than just designing some Print and Cancel buttons. Instead they set out to invent a symbolic writing system that communicates to the human precisely how the machine works, what is possible, and would also allow the machine to feed back what it was doing. And they imagined doing all of this through a concise symbolic graphic language. It was an impossible task.

One decision they immediately took was separating the graphics from the button, so that when you put your finger on the live area, you're not covering up the instructions.

Here's a drawing [↓].

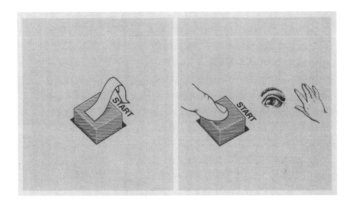

They proceeded from this first insight to develop a graphic visual language, attached as graphic labels which attempted to communicate what
the buttons allowed. The Power button [↙] label is the largest, and at top
right of the layout. Stop is bottom left, its label unlike the others. Start has
two labels [↘] for two functions, Transmit and Receive.

 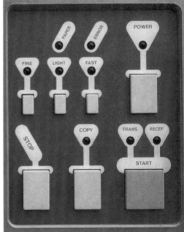

The first buttons were physical, but King and Miranda already knew
that completely flat panels with whole-surface sensitivity were going
to appear soon. And this was an even more critical kind of graphic
problem because you need to identify what places were touchable,
and what those touches would do. So they developed a more detailed
graphic language for these flat, transmitting, sensitive soft displays.
The graphic system they designed needed to work both with the hard

buttons and also evolve for the new, soft ones. So where graphic labels were lifted and separated from the hard buttons, with soft panels the labels remained offset from where a finger touches the machine. Physical buttons were replaced with groups of repeating horizontal bars, both graphically and tactilely articulated. Here is a production drawing for the soft buttons which shows a simple case [↙] as well as a more complicated control [↘].

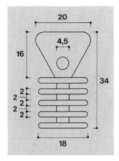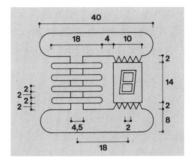

One thing that immediately struck me when I found this book was how these interfaces were photographed [↓], self-consciously and disembodied with their rainbow cables trailing plastic interface panels carefully styled and set against heavily patterned surfaces. This would have felt contemporary, synchronous as it was with the Memphis design movement, which traded in surface, ornament, and synthesis in a related way.

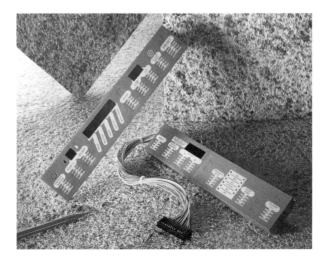

In the first lecture I described how the book expands from this discrete design project to the full sweep of human communication. It doesn't, however, very clearly detail how this graphic interface language really works. The book provides broad principles, but few details. The interface design project which was the reason for publishing *Design Interface* is presented only at the very end of the volume. The preceding chapters deal with interface in a much broader register, and I guess this is what I like so much about it. In the course, you're also dealing with a very constrained interface problem—the design of a clock face for the Apple Watch. But I believe you can use these tight assignments to address much larger problems. Perhaps only in a very small way, like the red key on a Lettera 22 typewriter, but design can then become more of a platform, or better, a lever.

"... Meet the Tetracono"

I want to talk about a design research project that I worked on for the first half of 2017. The main protagonist is Bruno Munari and this will focus on one particular work I find particularly rich.

In 1965, Italian artist and designer Bruno Munari released the Tetracono [↗] with an event and exhibition at the Danese Milano showroom, inviting spectators to—quote—"... meet the Tetracono," as if it was a person. But Tetracono is a product—an austere, 15-centimeter, black steel cube, housing four aluminum cones, each painted half red and half green, and designed to spin at four different distinct speeds on an 18-minute cycle. Its stated function was to show forms while they were in the process of becoming. My design research work around it included both historical research and also making things today. It was the result of six months spent as a design fellow at the American Academy in Rome, where I was given the time and space to investigate something. I'd been interested in this object for a good while and realized that I could talk about everything I wanted to talk about just through this one object. I also thought it'd be nice to spend six months looking at a 15-centimeter box.

So, the story begins around 1962. Munari was an artist, designer, writer, teacher, definitely an inventor, occasionally a curator. He was trained as an artist in Milan in the beginning of the 20th century. He associated himself with the Italian Futurists in the first quarter of the 20th century, but he came onto the movement late. And, in fact, he kind of quickly departed from some of their ideas.

He became increasingly disillusioned with fine art as a practice distinct from design or working in the world, at large, and was vocal about it. By 1962 he was writing a regular column in the Milan newspaper, *Il Giorno*. There, he called on his fellow artists to change their practice:

> Today it's become necessary to demolish the myth of the star artist.

He continues,

> Culture today is becoming a mass affair, and the artist must step down from his pedestal and be prepared to make a sign for a butcher's shop (if he knows how to do it).

That was a particularly blunt statement of what he had both implied and modeled throughout his career. This was the only way for art to again make contact with the public at large.

In order to do this applied art work—design which had as ambitious a scope as Munari thought it should—he needed sympathetic clients who would go along for the ride. One of these was Danese Milano, a design gallery and publisher based in Milan. It was established by Jacqueline Vodoz and Bruno Danese in 1952, and for the first several years they sold principally one-off ceramics. These objects were useful objects, but they were only ever made as unique objects, never produced in multiple copies. They were premised on the "touch of the artist" in some way.

In 1957, Bruno Danese sought out Munari, who was already working and had a significant reputation in Milan at the time. Danese invited Munari to make a project with him and Munari replied by saying something like, "OK, I'm happy to do that, happy to work with you, but I have this idea and it's very different than what you've already been doing. I have an idea for an ashtray. It's a cube-shaped ashtray, I've already designed it in my head. I'm not a smoker, and I find seeing butts in an ashtray unaesthetic. I want to solve that problem, and I have a good idea of how to solve it. But here's the thing. I think," as he says to Danese, "it's a time of industrial production and you're making these one-off things and calling them design. I want you to produce this product, to manufacture it in an industrial manner and circulate it through society, of course." And this is the product that resulted. It's called the Cubo ashtray [↓].

It's elegantly, simply made. It is two pieces [↗], a melamine plastic cube and a piece of aluminum bent in this certain way so as to collect and hide the cigarette ends. The Cubo ashtray was, at first, a commercial failure. A lot of money was spent on manufacturing it and it didn't sell very well—I don't know that people would have known to go to Danese's design showroom to find such a thing. But Danese was steadfast, he believed in the product, and remained committed to manufacturing it. It's still in production today, 50 years later; it's become a hit. In fact, when you buy the thing now, like I did when I was in Rome, it still says on the package:

> Bruno Danese who had been looking for Bruno Munari, put the ashtray into production and for a year or two it was decidedly unsuccessful. But with the insistence of Bruno Danese, and due to its essentiality, this ashtray is still sold today all over the world. Is it perhaps a "classic"?

Danese and Munari struck up an active working relationship. Munari got involved in many aspects of the business quickly, even suggesting other artists to collaborate with Danese. One of the first he suggested was Enzo Mari, a graphic designer based in Milan. He was a little bit younger than Munari and took an overtly ethical stance in his design work. Munari,

Mari, and Bruno Danese got involved in designing the showroom lay-outs and producing exhibitions. They'd stage exhibitions for products, like displays, where the visual rhetoric followed a consistent idea about industrial production—serial production, always in multiple copies, designed to be manufactured. And that went for everything from the look of the packages (brown paper cardboard with one-color printing) to the design of the showroom. So here is the basement of the Danese Milano store [↘], and that is a typical Danese shop layout at the time. It looks rather relentless, definitely repetitive, but also does a good job amplifying the serial production of these design objects.

Munari wrote about this idea of serial production concisely in a book that's not translated into English but is a superior collection of his work. It's called *Codice ovvio* (Obvious Code).

> Serial production is not reproduction. Reproduction implies that there is an original unique piece, which as such cannot be reproduced, but which production techniques try to imitate as closely as possible. Therefore, the reproduction is always inferior to the original and its main function as documentation. On the other hand, production uses the techniques which are available to the artist today to manufacture a given number of pieces, not copies without the existence of an original which can be the same or slightly different depending on the methods of production, design, planning, etc. The number of pieces produced varies according to the

techniques and the subjects involved from a minimum of fifty to an unlimited number in order to obtain more reasonable prices. Only those who mistake price for value are not interested in this type of production.

Serial production is different from reproduction, and a reproduction is always inferior to the original. The multiple was central to this logic.

This is an Enzo Mari graphic [↓] from a mid-1960s Danese catalog that picks up the thread. The composite image is made up of Danese products, each shown multiple times. The graphic itself was repeated in many settings, from an exhibition poster to a catalog cover to a postcard.

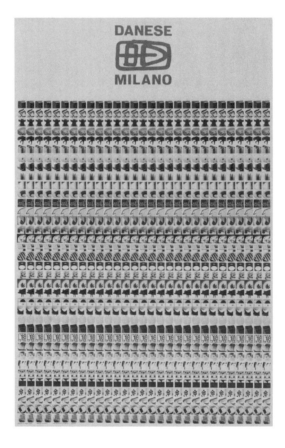

Munari continued to work with Danese to produce a couple of products, and in 1965 the Tetracono was released. Fifteen centimeters, a steel cube, with four aluminum cones inside. "It was designed explicitly to convey a philosophical attitude," he said, "to see the universe as an indivisible unit of pure energy, which is constantly undergoing transformations." This [↓] is the recipe for how the Tetracono is assembled. The starting point is a square, from which a hollow cube is constructed. Four interior faces each contain a cone with a base the size of a circle inscribed in that square. The area of each cone takes up three quarters of its area. The cone is painted half red and half green.

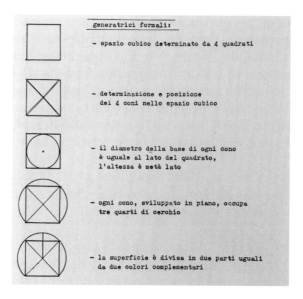

He also provided a script [↓], the program, for how this object behaves.

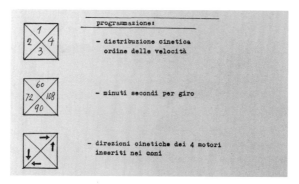

Munari's program lays out a speed distribution across the four cones. The top is fastest, then the other speeds follow counter-clockwise and the rotation speed of each cone is noted in seconds. So, you can see that the first cone turns once every 60 seconds. The second one down to the left turns once every 72 seconds. Then 90 seconds, and then 108. It turns out those numbers have a harmonic relationship to each other. They come into and out of phase in a regular pattern, which then gives the Tetracono exceptionally beautiful movement. Finally the last piece of the script details the direction of movement for the four cones. Two rotate up to the top right corner and other two rotate toward the opposite corner.

The first edition was built with motors and was more or less a total flop. Too expensive, too unreliable, and too few were made. The second edition was issued without motors. Tetracono SM was a bit more successful. The price was reasonable, and it was intended that you move the cones yourself. (I didn't really understand this when I started looking at the object.) Importantly, at the time, Danese Milano made no distinction in their catalogs between their art editions like this and their consumer products, like the ashtray. They were shown side-by-side, and so the Tetracono was presented as a product, if a fairly strange one.

Jump to 2017. I'd never seen a Tetracono working, I had only once seen a Tetracono in person—I'd borrowed one for an exhibition—but had never seen one moving, and I still didn't know very much about it.

Arriving in Rome with a lot of time and space to think about something and having an outline of the project I wanted to do, I thought the best way to just start was to make a paper model. And since I had Munari's instructions, I thought, why not? It would be productive to just assemble a little model to understand what it looks like, what it feels like. This [↙] is the master drawing which I cut and assembled leaving in the construc-tion lines.

The Tetracono is a marginal Munari project. There isn't much known about it and not many images exist. So, I just started collecting things that seemed relevant, one of which was *Opera aperta* by Umberto Eco and designed by Munari from right about that time. And the cone found its way onto that.

I was discovering (or remembering, perhaps) that by simply starting to make things, those things will help you look around at what's immediate and see differently [↑]. Spending my first significant amount of time in Rome, I was then starting to understand Munari in his Italian context, connecting the classical geometry of the Tetracono to, say, the Pantheon with its oculus hole in the ceiling and perfect hemisphere dome [↙],

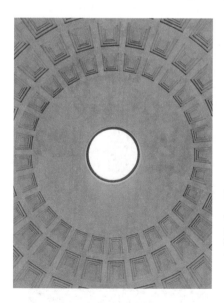 

or looking out the studio window [↗] at the symmetry of the fountain, or this forced perspective [↙] by Francesco Borromini or [↘] a tiled floor.

The next step was to realize Munari's script. I'd never seen a Tetracono moving and so I set to making a software model. I left it running in the studio, interested to understand if I might grasp how the pattern changes over time. Could I recognize a repeat if exposed to it for long enough? Would I start to read temporal patterns in more complex, holistic ways? As before, making something causes you to look around at the world differently. I saw the Tetracono elsewhere, in a table top [↙] on an overnight ferry and again in a church courtyard [↘].

I was almost convinced that any of these static arrangements would start moving as well, shift in time.

* * *

The next stop was a basement in Milan. I figured the best thing to do with this was to actually get my hands on a Tetracono and try to work with it. After making the software model, I had the idea to make a stop-motion video using still photographs of the object, which I would put together and make run. But I needed to find an actual Tetracono to work with to do this.

Through a number of contacts, I found a collector with a Tetracono who was generous enough to invite me to Milan to work with his. He met me at the train station and we drove out to the northeastern corner of the city. We arrived at a high rise residential building, walked down a set of steps in the rear to a basement, where he led me to his space, and opened the door. The space was filled with a large and detailed collection of 20th-century Italian product design. The Tetracono was out and ready.

I set up my camera and lights [↑] and made a sequence of still photographs of the Tetracono so that I could assemble the object moving. My first visit was a scouting mission and proof of concept to make sure the result would look good.

Here's a very rough first version [↓].

I quickly realized that I needed more photos to make the full sequence. And so I returned to Rome to work out from the software model where the edge of the red and green should be at any one moment.

I then used that information to produce a kind of temporal diagram [↙].

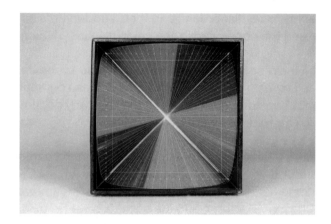

The diagram could then be overlaid on my live camera feed to tell where to put the edge of the red and green, and when. When I returned to Milan, I spent the day lining up the cones to match my diagram, using the image on the screen as a larger viewfinder and moving each cone a tiny bit at a time with my finger to get it in the right place. It was nearly impossible. In that shoot, I made a comprehensive series of photographs which you see here on a contact sheet [↓]. I then produced five takes of the entire sequence, which I assembled later with video software.

The thing I noticed in living with the Tetracono is that it goes through very recognizable moments of transformation. At the end, right before it turns to green, it seems to be discordant, and then, suddenly it's as if it all clicks in at one time and the cones are all one color. It's kind of magical.

The next place the research led me was to the Fondazione Jacqueline Vodoz e Bruno Danese, in Milan, which is the Danese company archive. I told them what I was doing and asked if they had any documentation on the Tetracono. They did, so I went back to Milan.

The foundation is in an old apartment in a palazzo in the center of Milan. And it is beautiful. It was renovated in the 1990s by Achille Castiglioni; a wonderful combination of old and new [↙]. The company was recently sold to a lighting manufacturer, and the collection was in mild disrepair. It had a charming ad hoc quality. For example, when you walk in the door, there's an odd semi-circular canvas, a Munari painting, that he made explicitly for that spot [↘].

I wanted to look at the printed material around the Tetracono. I found two small Tetracono brochures, one of which announced the Tetracono as a product, and the other which announced an exhibition and product launch. I was surprised to see that one of the main images was a 35mm filmstrip of the object changing colors. I shouldn't have been surprised though, because the essence of the Tetracono is how it changes. The product brochure describes the product, listing its size, but it also does something characteristically Munari. He gives the spatial dimension as 15 × 15 × 15 centimeters. He also gives the mass, and then finally the *temporal dimension* of the object as 1080 seconds. The Tetracono has both spatial and temporal dimensions—perfect.

The original [↑] of Munari's recipe diagram for the Tetracono was in the archive. As was one of the motorized versions [↑]; the only one that seems to be in working order, and I was excited to see it move. The motorized Tetracono is larger at 20 × 20 × 20 centimeters and sits on a base which holds the electrical equipment.

We unpacked it but we couldn't find the power cord. The archivist found it a bit later that evening, plugged it in, started it up, and sent me a video. What I noticed immediately was that the Tetracono was running, yes, but, based on everything I had uncovered, it was running incorrectly according to Munari's program. Two cones (bottom left and bottom) should have been moving in towards each other, and the other two (top and top right) likewise. Instead, three cones were all moving in one direction and one was moving in a different direction. They're also not moving at the right rates. I relayed the news immediately and made plans to return.

On returning, we confirmed the fact that it was, in fact, counter to the way that Munari intended. The archivist had been working with the foundation for a long time and was involved when this Tetracono had been "renovated" about 14 years earlier for a show at the Museo del Novecento. She found the documentation and, as we suspected, when it was fixed, it was fixed improperly. She knew the person who worked on it and called him. He's retired since, but his workshop exists and between them they decided, yes, this should definitely be corrected.

Three months later, the Tetracono was fixed and is now running correctly. So my design research project then accidentally became a historic preservation project [↓].

Tetracono di Munari, smontato per la revisione dei motori

Next, I wanted to know how the objects were manufactured. I learned that the Tetracono was made in the studio of Gruppo T. I set up an interview with Giovanni Anceschi, the group's founder. He spoke about how the object came to be. At the time Anceschi was working closely with Munari. He had a studio together with the other members of Gruppo T, and Munari would often use the studio for its manufacturing capabilities (they had a small lathe and metal working tools). The Tetracono was manufactured by an outside metal craftsperson in the studio.

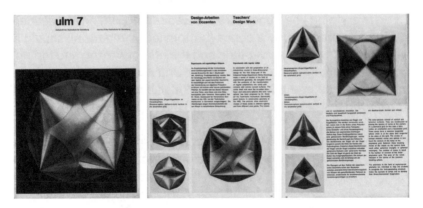

But in the interview, Anceschi began talking about where the idea for the Tetracono originated [↑]. At the time, he was a student at Ulm school of design. Anceschi would travel back from Ulm to Milan on weekends, carrying ideas and printed matter back to share with his friends, including Munari. *Ulm* 7 featured a design research project by Walter Zeischegg that's a morphological study of cones, spheres, and cubes. Both Munari and Anceschi loved it.

The final stop in this extended investigation was an "industrial artisan" screen printer in Umbria. I didn't have an idea in mind to produce, but it quickly seemed right to think about a print, or prints, of the Tetracono. An initial idea was to simply make four different large silkscreen prints which all looked roughly the same but were actually different moments in the Tetracono's color transformation. I discussed this with Stuart Bertolotti-Bailey, and we somehow arrived at the idea of combining all four states into one print. "Industrial artisan" is an interestingly contradictory description, and for screen printing this simply means that there is a machine and a person who has to register every print by hand. I love that contradiction in relation to how Munari talks about production. Screen printing works by laying down one color at a time—cyan, magenta, yellow, and black in sequence. A photographic image lets only some of the ink pass through the screen [↓].

As we see here, the machine is running and printing directly on the paper and being aligned by hand [↓].

The idea for the combined print was simply to use that production process of cyan, magenta, yellow, and black, then take the 18 minutes of the Tetracono cycle and divide it by four to arrive at four distinct states in Tetracono's sequence. So, the cyan plate would be at three minutes, the yellow plate would be at six minutes, magenta at nine minutes, and black at twelve minutes. Each of these colors is overprinted one at a time in sequence with drying time between. Cyan [↙] was the first plate, magenta was the second plate [↓], then yellow [↘],

and finally black. The result is this almost psychedelic Tetracono with colors that never existed in the original [↓].

The print attempts a kind of "time sandwich," a representation of a longer moment in one static image. We included a key [↓] at the bottom of the sheet borrowed from Munari, and marks were added to register the time of each color.

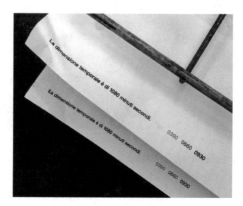

At the end of this meandering design research project, I was left with many thoughts about serial production, working in multiples, and what makes sense currently in relation to these ideas which are themselves quite old. And it occurred to me that now, 50 years later, we've moved on from industrial production of objects to the post-industrial production of information: from cubic ashtrays to bespoke emojis. And it made me consider that the Tetracono was in many ways already a post-industrial product. Or perhaps both industrial and post-industrial at once. It was a manufactured object of steel and aluminum, but its purpose was to produce a constantly changing image. Its rhetorical design was in its script: how the cones turn, the sequence, the phasing, its temporal dimension. Munari called it both a product for exploring programming and an object for understanding forms in the process of becoming. Both of these lessons seem equally, or maybe more, important now than they did in 1965.

Touch Start to Begin

This is a case study of an interface designed over 20 years ago and still in use today, fundamentally unchanged. This is a project I worked on, so it will have some personal detail.

We begin in 1995. I had just started working at IDEO San Francisco for Bill Moggridge. Here he is speaking at the White House [↓].

IDEO was a product design firm, but around that time they'd moved into the new practice of interaction design. I'd worked for a couple years in New York, and had heard about what was going on at IDEO. It sounded exciting and I managed to get a job there as an interaction designer. I moved to California.

Twelve years before in 1983, Moggridge designed this laptop computer, the Grid Compass [↓]. Laptops were novel and, as I understand it, when Moggridge began to live with the machine he soon realized that the bulk of his attention was focused on the screen. The physical design of the product was good, but the interface was where the action was. This epiphany at least in part led to developing interaction design at IDEO. By 1995, when I arrived, the discipline was established, if fairly new.

This is a New York City subway token [↙], also from 1995. The token came from a clerk in a subway station booth [↘]. You walked up to the booth, stuffed your dollar under the window, and said, "One." A token was returned and that token then put into a slot in a turnstile, which let you enter the subway. It was fast, could be a bit gruff, but it was quite efficient.

At the time, the MTA (Metropolitan Transit Authority) was moving away from tokens and would soon introduce the MetroCard, a magnetic swipe stored value system, for fare payment. The MetroCard uses card readers built into turnstiles to validate transactions. Although you could also buy your MetroCard from the token booth, the MTA would soon offer an electronic vending machine for purchasing a MetroCard via a touch-screen interface. The new machine would eventually make the token booth redundant. There'd still be a clerk there to manage questions and problems and hand out maps, but most of the cards were meant to be sold through the machine. The MTA had been working on this project for a while already, but the machine was delayed. The job was commissioned to Cubic Westinghouse, a defense and public transportation contractor based in San Diego who was already building turnstiles and station furni-ture for the MTA. You might imagine that Cubic Westinghouse didn't have a great deal of experience, or design nuance anyway, for the electronic, user-facing aspects of this new machine which facilitates a rather com-plicated transaction.

Design for screens was also still relatively crude and computer interfaces were not ubiquitous in the same way they are now. To get an idea of that context, Google was not even the glimmer of an idea yet. And a web browser (Netscape Version 1.0) looked like this [↓].

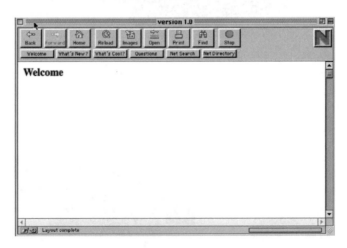

Although Cubic Westinghouse had the design-build contract to both design the machines and also manufacture them, they had not produced a convincing prototype. At what seems to have been the last minute, the MTA called in IDEO who was already known for this kind of work—product design, interaction design, and projects that merged the two. The MTA is a large government agency with stretched budgets and the fees reflected this. The project timeline was very short. This was not a typical IDEO commission.

I was young, enthusiastic, had just moved from New York, and recognized the potential of this project to have a mass impact. Industrial designer Masamichi Udagawa was much more experienced, but he also immediately saw the potential when we started to work on the project together. (I expect the condensed timeline and relatively low fees must have been part of the reason why I was put on the project.) IDEO had previously designed a touchscreen interface for the London Underground, so I soon left for IDEO's London office to learn from its designer, Kathleen Holman, and to work on this new interface.

Meanwhile, Masamichi moved to New York to establish IDEO New York. Exiled between my desk in a London attic space and Masamichi's New York apartment, the project moved ahead in relative isolation. Before IDEO, Masamichi was working as an industrial designer at Apple, where he designed a series of PowerBook laptops, among other projects. He was more seasoned and already intimately acquainted with complex hardware/software design problems. He directed the project as the lead industrial designer. I followed his direction, with my work focused on the interface.

Before the project was complete and the machines installed four years later, Masamichi, together with Sigi Möslinger, established Antenna Design, a product and interaction design studio that has since made exceptional work for clients including the MTA, Knoll, and Bloomberg, designing everything from trains to screens to furniture. Here they are sometime closer to now [↓].

My first real design job was at Two Twelve Associates, a graphic design firm in New York that had worked on an early touchscreen interface for

Citibank ATMs which was quite successful and distinct. That project was led by studio principle Sylvia Harris [↙]. Together with classmates David Gibson [↓], and Juanita Dugdale [↘], Harris formed Two Twelve Associates as a graphic design studio whose explicit focus was large public design projects. Although I didn't get to work on that project, the office was an exceptionally nurturing environment and I was able to observe Harris and others at work on it.

The Citibank ATM that resulted was a first-person interface, addressing the user directly. The interaction started with, "Hello. May I help you?" and then continued to guide a user through the banking process, confirming each step along the way. It was an example of good, clear public interface design [↓].

When we started work on the MetroCard Automated Vending Machine project, a sequence of screens was already in place. We began by questioning that order and considering alternatives in the flow. The user paths (flows) were complicated and there were a number of possible transactions that the new machine would implement, including buying a multi-ride card, a single ride ticket, adding value to an existing card, and even trading in and consolidating cards. Here's a page from the initial spec document [↓].

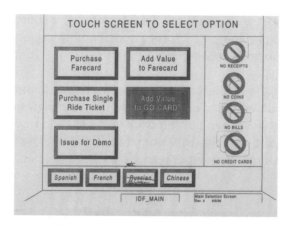

A primary goal for the MetroCard interaction was to make the transaction as efficient as possible. Buying a token was a quick, scripted maneuver. It was something you did over and over and over again. So we set several competing conceptual models for how the touchscreen interface would work. These are listed in a drawing here [↓].

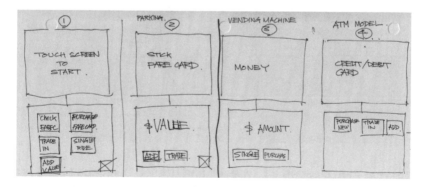

The first model was just the existing flow. Number 2 was based on a parking lot interaction where the user first inserts a card and then adds value to it. Number 3 was the "Vending Machine"—think of a snack or soda vending machine. The first thing you do when you walk up to the machine is insert money. Then you choose potato chips, press one button, and the potato chips come out. Done. The final model was a more elaborate transaction, based on a bank machine interface. We called it the "ATM." In that interaction, you walk up to the machine and it says, "Oh, do you want to do something? Put in your card. OK? Now type in your PIN." And it continues, "Now here are the things that you can do today." And you choose one option, press the button, the interface confirms, "Do you want to do that?" You confirm, "Yes." The interaction continues guiding the user step-by-step through the process with confirmations at each decision point along the way. This is a considerably longer transaction process, but also quite reassuring.

After identifying these interaction models, we began to arrange the existing flow of screens provided by the MTA to match these approaches. These drawings were then passed back to the MTA to review. These were adjusted, and new flows resubmitted. It was an iterative process. Here's part of a large working drawing [↓].

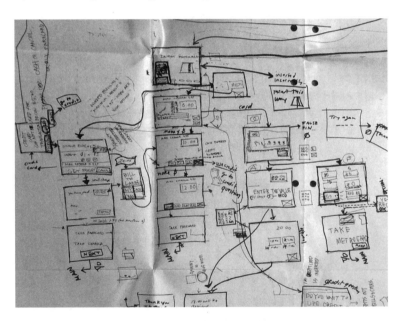

These were then cleaned up, typeset, and passed back again. The process went back and forth with Masamichi directing our work, but it was also remarkably efficient. This was likely helped by the fact that we had one principal advocate at the MTA and Masamichi handled all of the communication directly in New York. We converted these flows into two software prototypes to match the Vending Machine and ATM interaction models that the MTA then put in front of a small group of users.

Overwhelmingly, users responded to the ATM interaction model. The new vending machine was somehow confusing, and it was certainly new, to these test users. Now, I thought the Vending Machine was clearly the way to go as it would be faster, more immediate, and cleaner. But turns out I had totally the wrong instinct. Now I'd guess that given the novelty of this transaction—an interaction model that guided a user through the process, spoke directly to the user, and confirmed each step along the way—was both more understandable and more comfortable. So, we proceeded with the ATM.

The user base was extraordinarily wide: people using it for the first time, people using it for the 5,000th time, people visiting New York, young people, old people, in all sorts of conditions, speaking many languages. The interface needed to be absolutely direct. The touchscreen was small, constrained to 832 × 624 pixels, and so the graphics also couldn't be complicated. There was a lot to fit in and a quick idea for the screen layout appeared where horizontal bands could house different types of information. Those types were: Regulatory (what rules are in effect), Status (where you are in the process), Instruction (what to do next), and Global (system-wide options like cancel or language). By placing these in consistent locations, we hoped that this might ground the experience. The horizontal-only division of screen real estate also indicated a kind of direction to the interface. Here's another sketch which shows what I'm describing [↓].

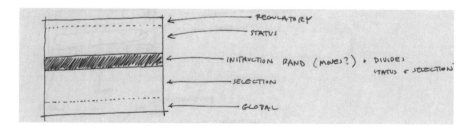

The central graphic idea of the interface then emerged from this layout. A strong yellow instruction bar moves from top to bottom down the interface as the MetroCard transaction progresses. The bar addresses the user directly with clear instructions.

Below the bar is the active selection area, comprised of a series of buttons for equivalent choices. Above the bar is status, what the user has already selected. Conceptually, the bar is the present, below the bar is the future, and above the bar is the past. At the end of the transaction, the bar says, "Thank you," wipes the screen from bottom to top returning to the rest state—"Touch start to begin." [↓]

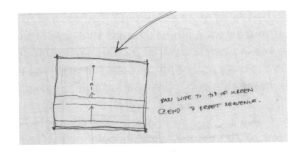

The physical hardware was already configured to accommodate the components, including the touchscreen, when the project started, but it was not yet detailed and so allowed some flexibility. Masamichi was the industrial designer and leading the project. I was tasked with the interface design. We immediately had ideas about ways to merge the two, blur the line between the hardware and the software. (This was common practice at IDEO at the time.) We imagined that what happens on screen could be color-coded to the related physical areas of the machine including cash entry, credit card swipe, receipt printing, and MetroCard delivery. Here's a drawing of the hardware color coding [↓].

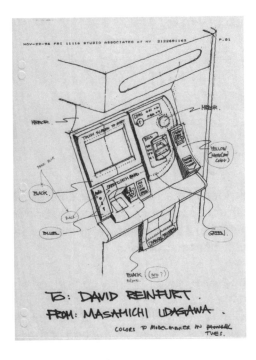

When the on-screen bar delivered instructions, its background color would shift to correspond to the area on the machine that you touch or use at that point in the process. So if it instructs the user to, "Take your MetroCard," then the bar is yellow and that matches the yellow area where your MetroCard comes out. Or when it asks you to insert cash, the bar is green, matching the green bill acceptor on the machine.

There was already an existing graphic language for the interface and no compelling reason to depart from that. In 1970, Vignelli Associates designed a robust graphic system for the MTA [↙] still being used today. We worked directly from the MTA Graphic Standards Manual [↘] and it laid out the choices unambiguously.

The machine also needed to be used by people whose vision was impaired. The Americans with Disabilities Act provided some guidance, but we needed more and so we turned to the Lighthouse, an organization for partially sighted people that advocates accessibility in public spaces. Working with the Lighthouse New York office, we learned some surprising things about the population of partially sighted people in the city. An extremely small percentage read Braille. There are many shades of sightedness, and to call somebody blind or not is a threshold rather than a binary reckoning. Most people have at least some vision and there are certain choices which particularly help legibility. One of the most important was contrast. Size was also quite important. We decided to use these as criteria for the interface design. Color was also useful, and distinguishing between colors was quite possible with impaired sight.

We made made further software models and put these again in front of users coordinated by the MTA. This was a fairly early version of the interface. You see the bars start coming down the screen, you choose "new card," you choose how many rides you want, you see when the card moves up there it has the notch taken out of it, you choose "cash," you put in your money, do you want a receipt, yes or no, take change, take receipt, and then it wipes the screen and goes back to the beginning. From that prototype [↘] there was an immediate response: the buttons don't look enough like buttons.

Completely fair. I started into a bunch of graphic studies to work out how to make a button that would look more like a "button" but also remain starkly graphic, coherent with the rest of the interface. I was reluctant to make floating buttons that glowed when pressed—this was a common tendency at the time. These studies [↓] imagine the three-dimensional consequences of certain graphic, two-dimensional choices. The drawing reminds me that interface design trades heavily in metaphor, and so choices for how an object in the interface *looks* has corresponding implications for what the object *is supposed to be,* and therefore how it should behave.

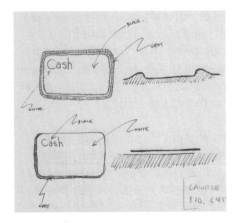
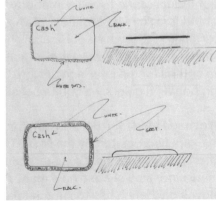

The eventual winner was the one on the right [↓].

The interface doesn't work that differently, although when you choose cards they are without the notch before you have selected one, then it moves to the top and gets the graphic notch. That's a small thing, but also an interface lives and dies in the details and their coherence as a visual and interaction language.

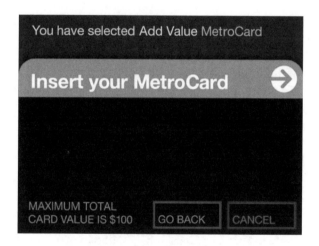

A slightly evolved version here [↑]. I think increasingly the MTA was concerned about the complications of single ride cards, the add value transactions, and timed cards which did not yet exist. We committed a good bit of work to interfaces that would work with all of these. The point was to design a solution that addressed both what they were doing right now and also what they wanted to do in the future.

And, in fact, I would say that, in the interface, the driving criteria for me was just simply that it would *continue to function over time.* I was quite aware that this was going to be a project where once we handed it back to the MTA, and then back to Cubic Westinghouse, it would still get lots of input and likely change considerably. Sometimes when you work on design projects, your contract ends but the project continues and the final result turns out basically nothing like what you had designed. This is particularly true for bigger projects with more people involved and more at stake.

Throughout the interface design language, decisions were simple and modular enough that they might be able to be added to and changed. Over time this interface would need to evolve to add new languages, new dollar amounts, new sequences, etc. So, if the design was blunt, simple, even coarse, then it would also be more flexible in the future. To this end, the type size was very big, huge for what you might find on a screen at the time. Colors were kept modest. The screen layout was never fussy. And the graphic devices that pulled the interface together were kept simple enough that additional demands on the language, or sequence, or even function would not destroy its gestalt.

Six months in, and we finally arrived at a modeled prototype for the machine itself, together with an interactive demo for its interface. The model was skeletal, only a front face rendered in fiberglass and only certain paths of the interface were built out in the software. That model was staged in an anonymous tower in midtown Manhattan where a testing coordinator [↙] led approximately 30 people through the steps of using the prototype machine.

We'd rented a touchscreen to wire into the demo, but (predictably) it didn't work. As you can see [↗], we stacked a CRT monitor on reams of paper to fit the opening on the model. A mouse cord extended from the computer to a small table next to it. Masamichi sat at the mouse and clicked wherever the user would touch the screen. I was behind a two-way mirror, watching and listening. Apparently, the illusion was convincing and the feedback conclusive. We didn't change much after that.

In the meantime, the project finished for me and I went back to graduate school in 1997. I delivered a folder of .pict final graphic assets and comprehensive layouts for each of the screens and the MetroCard Automated Vending Machine went back to Cubic Westinghouse for the next two years to code the software and build the hardware. Meanwhile, I continued to struggle through graduate school with passing thoughts about the project and hearing an occasional update from Masamichi, whose new firm continued to work with the MTA. By 1999, the machines were ready and the first was installed at the 68th Street/Hunter College station on January 26, 1999. It appeared in the *New York Times* that day [↘] and I went to see the finished machine and to use it.

A Subterranean Automaton
Carrie Boretz for The New York Times
A Metrocard machine was hauled into the subway station at 68th Street and Lexington Avenue yesterday. Ten of the machines, which will accept cash, credit cards and debit cards in exchange for subway passes, will go into operation on Monday. Page B3.

I was shocked—the interface design intent was largely intact, as was the physical machine. The finished product was almost exactly like what we sent. And it was good.

Since the first machines were installed, the interface has evolved but the graphics have stayed the same. Sequences have adjusted, words changed, functions were added and removed, but the interface remains in use at the time of writing. This project confirmed my strong belief about thinking through how what you are designing will change over time, knowing that it will, and trying to design that knowledge into the solution. Radio Frequency ID (RFID) contactless payment tickets have just been introduced in New York and the MetroCard machine will be phased out soon enough. Still, 20-something years is a pretty long run for an interface.

Desktops, Trashcans

This follows the work of two interface designers, Muriel Cooper and Susan Kare, both seen previously. When looking at interfaces I find it particularly useful to look at things that are out of date, that don't clearly register in the current moment. It's even better if these are from long enough ago that we've forgotten what screens looked like then. Interface design and graphic conventions both change and also cohere incredibly fast, so this isn't hard.

Interface design is an explicitly speculative exercise, and so when looking at interfaces from the past we see what the present was supposed to look like. Sometimes these match our current situation, but often they don't. In either case, the speculative interface design scenarios reveal desires for how we'd like our computers to behave. The fictions suggest uses we may have never known we wanted, but by articulating these as rendered design proposals, they often end up directly forming the interfaces we end up with.

I'd like to look at a few of these interface design scenarios from a print and television campaign run by AT&T in 1993 called "You Will." The ads describe and render a collection of interfaces coming sometime in the near future. At the time, these looked impossibly futuristic, but now, more than 20 years later, many, even most, are intimately familiar.

AT&T Ad 1: Have you ever borrowed a book from thousands of miles away? Crossed the country without stopping for directions? Or sent someone a fax from the beach? You will. And the company that will bring it to you, AT&T.

AT&T Ad 2: Have you ever paid a toll without slowing down? Bought concert tickets from cash machines? Or tucked your baby in from a phone booth? You will. And the company that'll bring it to you, AT&T.

AT&T Ad 3: Have you ever opened doors with the sound of your voice? Carried your medical history in your wallet? Or attended a meeting in your bare feet? You will, and the company that will bring it to you, AT&T.

AT&T Ad 4: Have you ever watched the movie you wanted to the minute you wanted to? Learned special things from faraway places? Or tucked your baby in from a phone booth? You will, and the company that will bring it to you, AT&T.

What strikes me in watching these is that when working in interface design, the most consequential work doesn't have a template—there's no existing model. There are incremental advances in interface design perpetually put forward, like a better button design or a smoother loading widget, but these are driven more by a previous product than a comprehensive reimagination. The incremental designs respond to an existing interaction, rather than asking the more fundamental question of what the interaction could be. An interface can be radically reconceived, even just its visual vocabulary can suggest a completely different use. And this is what I like about both Muriel Cooper's and Susan Kare's work—neither had a model, so the work is original. Here's one more [↓], a print ad which is particularly relevant.

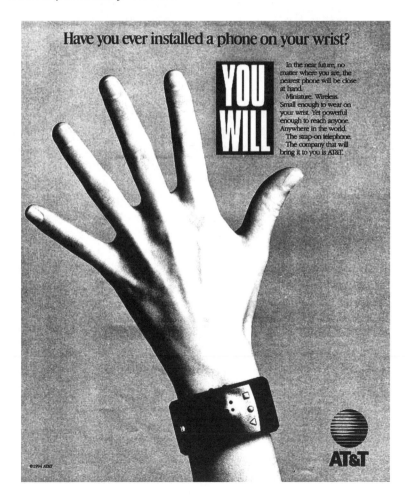

* * *

This is Muriel Cooper [↓] speaking at the 1994 TED conference in Monterey, California.

It was the fifth edition of the Technology, Entertainment, and Design conference founded by information architect Richard Saul Wurman, a close friend and colleague of Cooper's. The TED conference drew heavy hitters from the overlapping worlds described in its title. Cooper was there to show the most recent interface design work coming out of the Visible Language Workshop in the MIT Media Lab, which she directed. Muriel Cooper's loose but lucid TED talk looks a thousand miles away from the stage-managed, rehearsed, slick, and clickable TED talks on the internet today.

> **Muriel Cooper:** Thank you. I have a couple of—can you hear me? I have a couple of personal things in characteristic with the TED philosophy. First of all, I'm testing the boundaries to see how truly comfortable one can make oneself here.

She takes off her shoes and continues,

> Our goal has been for a very long time to try to examine in the so-called emerging technologies what the new form and content of design, of communication, might be. And to that end for many years we have been building sort of prototype visualization tools that would allow us to do something that seems relatively intuitive in order to say "What if we did this, then what would happen?" but to really visualize this stuff in as tight and iterative loop as we possibly could. So we're looking for the new design principles, umm, we're not at all sure what they are ...

The talk proceeds in a knockabout fashion as Cooper and her student, David Small, eventually launch into a live demonstration of Information Landscapes, the most recent, and most exciting, work in the Visible Language Workshop. The software demo also goes around in circles a bit, but the work was overwhelmingly convincing to the audience. Spontaneous applause, and even an audible gasp or two, punctuated the presentation. Afterwards, audience member Bill Gates requested a copy, the work appeared on the cover of the design trade magazine *I.D.*, with an article by Janet Abrams, and speaking requests piled up. This work seemed to be everywhere when I was working as a young interaction designer at IDEO San Francisco at the time. I'd like to come back to this work in a minute, but first some background.

Muriel Cooper worked at Massachusetts Institute of Technology in various capacities over 40 years. MIT at the time was an overwhelmingly male and technical environment, and this made her work all the more difficult and important. Cooper asserted herself within this homogenous, community. Here's a picture [↓] capturing a not unusual scene.

After time with the University Office of Design Services, a Fulbright scholarship, and a brief freelance career, Cooper was invited to design a logo for what would become MIT Press. The Technology Press was rebranding and its director asked Paul Rand to recommend a graphic designer to work with. Rand suggested Cooper, and what she landed on is still in use more than 50 years later. She continued to work for MIT Press and soon became its first Design and Media Director. There Cooper oversaw a stream of books bridging a group of related subjects, including architecture, urban planning, sociology, biology, media studies, and computer programming. The subjects left an impression. *Soft Architecture Machines* by Nicholas Negroponte [↙], detailed early attempts with MIT architecture students to apply the computer to design tasks.

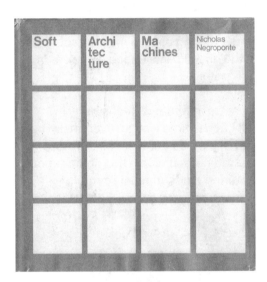 

Cooper and Negroponte were MIT colleagues and became close friends. This book continued a conversation around computers, interfaces, and design which began when Cooper attended Negroponte's FORTRAN programming class. Here [↗] she is with Donis A. Dondis rendered as ASCII art for a class assignment.

By 1974, she also started teaching in the Department of Architecture, offering a class together with Ron MacNeil called Messages and Means. It was popular and soon evolved into a constellation of courses set in a functioning classroom-studio hybrid they named the Visible Language Workshop. VLW courses were hands-on, centered around an offset printing press, a photographic darkroom, and increasingly, mini-computers, which were a rare resource in any design setting. Cooper was both fascinated by and inevitably frustrated by computers. She never learned to program, always felt the machines were too slow, or too clunky, or even downright hostile to their users. This antagonism, however, was productive and led her to imagine new interfaces where the digital tools would be as responsive and fluid as she desired. You get a sense of her

relationship with these digital tools by reading the caption to this photo [↙]
from a project by VLW student Nathan Felde.

Muriel is crazy. She's pounding away at the keyboard of a fifth generation,
laser-output, electrostatic, computer-driven, digital phototypesetter that
doesn't work. But that's okay. This is a research environment and the tools
aren't supposed to work. You're supposed to work. Besides, if you're
not making mistakes you probably aren't learning anything. And if you
can't make enough mistakes to learn anything there's nothing like a broken
machine to help you along. Muriel runs this place or should we say (after
that last thought), this place runs her. So if you want to get involved you
should listen to her closely.

In the first years of the VLW, she was already asking many of the interface questions that she and her students elegantly answered later.

For example, this simple video assignment [↓] asks what happens on a screen, or anyway, what should or could.

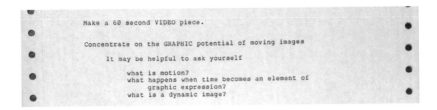

Make a 60 second VIDEO piece.

Concentrate on the GRAPHIC potential of moving images

It may be helpful to ask yourself

what is motion?
what happens when time becomes an element of
graphic expression?
what is a dynamic image?

By 1978, Cooper and Negroponte, together with psychologist Richard Bolt, were collaborating on a proposal for new computer interface research called "Books Without Pages." As its title suggests, the proposal asks what happens to the book when it moves on screen?

Although the National Science Foundation funding didn't work, this project collected many interface design ideas that Cooper went on to develop. Some found form in a video called Spatial Data Management System from 1980. SDMS was an imagined interface, environmental in its scale and immersive in its media. It was housed in a purpose-built room at MIT with a seamless rear-projection screen. The setup had touchscreens, a trackpad, even voice control. The main interface uses an expanded desktop metaphor, but instead of windows collecting documents, the documents were the objects themselves. It was a direct manipulation and zooming interface where opening a document simply scaled its contents [↓].

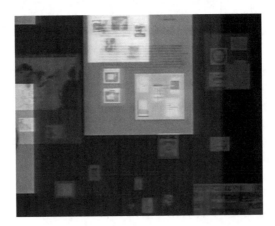

The team was also interested in how you could represent long documents. "A book has heft and weight," Cooper would say, and you just don't get that immediately with a digital document. They developed a compensating solution—the virtual page turn [↓], used as a graphic device to communicate moving through a long document and articulating it as so many sequential pages. Apple borrowed this page-turn for the first iPad. Others developed the infinite zoom for use in geographic data.

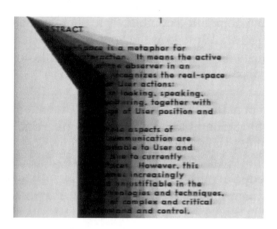

A computer is very low-resolution compared to the printed page and this makes type difficult to read on screen. Cooper and the VLW were consistently involved in trying to improve this situation. They knew we'd be reading on the screen more and more and it would no longer be just a case of getting something out of the computer, but rather the computer would become the experience. Negroponte's Architecture Machine Group had previously developed an approach to anti-aliasing type [↙] on a screen which made it easier to read.

that's

ANTI−ALIAS: A technique for smoothing graphics on a com-puter screen. The grid of a pixel−based display results in curves represented as discrete steps. By using a range of intermediate pixel values between foreground and background, these discrete steps can be rendered as smooth transitions. It is particularly important for typography where legibility is paramount.

The Visible Language Workshop continued to develop and refine this idea by digitizing a series of bitmap fonts and producing experiments in on-screen typography, considering how to make it more legible and what would be different on screen and in print.

It's important to know that Muriel Cooper turned away from print design in her mid-50s and committed completely to screen-based interface design work, a pretty bold move at the time. It was difficult territory, maybe not so satisfying because you could do so little on it, but she was convinced that's this is what all her other work led to.

An ongoing project at the VLW was called the "Ultimate Designer Workstation." From around 1988 until 1994, Cooper, MacNeil, and VLW students attempted to imagine and model what physical and electronic set up would be necessary for a graphic designer of the future to have the tools she needed at her disposal, both on- and off-screen, what kind of input devices would be relevant [↓], and what metaphors would be employed.

Another project the Visible Language Workshop attempted to model a visual programming language, one where you can see the structure of a computer program and manipulate its logic by adjusting its form. A software tool by Henry Lieberman used interlocking geometric shapes to communicate the structure of a computer program.

Cooper was consistently frustrated by the lack of any visual access to computer programming and this project was one attempt to fix that.

However, I'm not so sure that these three-dimensional diagrams solved the problem [↓].

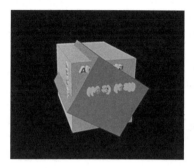 

I'd like to come back to the TED talk we started—with Muriel Cooper and David Small presenting Information Landscapes, the then-current work of the Visible Language Workshop. The demo included work by David Small, Suguru Ishizaki, Lisa Strausfeld, and Earl Rennison. Information Landscapes imagined a three-dimensional typographic environment where the user navigates by pointing their mouse and moving through this space, reading as they go. The project suggested a radically different computer interface than what existed, but one anchored in typographic and perspectival conventions evolved over 500 years. Relationships between contents were described by relative proximity and positions in three-dimensional space. Blur was used to facilitate legibility.

This ground-exploding work was never substantially extended. Muriel Cooper died unexpectedly six months after debuting this material at age 68. Although it was well represented within the design community, there wasn't a driving force to keep it moving. It remains an alternate speculative future for interface design [↓].

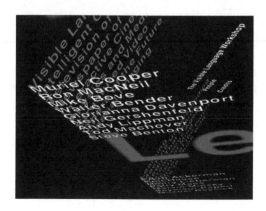

Earlier, she had already seen its possibility:

> I was convinced the line between reproduction tools and design would
> blur when information became electronic and that the lines between
> designer and artist, author and designer, professional and amateur, would
> also dissolve.

* * *

Now let's look at Susan Kare. Like Muriel Cooper, she also came into
interface design without the heavy baggage of existing models. Kare was
an artist with a PhD working in San Francisco when she was recruited
to join the original Apple Macintosh team. In the push to produce this
new "computer for the rest of us" which used a graphic user interface,
mouse, keyboard, and point and click navigation, it was increasingly
apparent that the graphic interface not only needed to operate intuitively,
but it also needed to communicate intuitively. In fact, those distinctions
are less crisp than they first appear. To operate smoothly, the on-screen
choices and metaphors had to be understandable, distinct, and memorable, even elegant.

Here's the core Macintosh team in a pyramid. Kare [↓] is at top right.

She arrived in Cupertino without prejudice as to what this new computer
interface should look like. In a 2018 speech, she described the scenario:

Making mosaic ashtrays was probably my earliest foray into digital design. Maybe there's just something about arranging tiles and squares. My high school friend Andy Hertzfeld who was working at Apple, he needed some graphic design help. I thought, sure, I can give it a shot. He showed me a prototype Macintosh. A graphical user interface allowed people that didn't know anything about computers to get a computer to do something. I represented the target audience. I was a sole source of it, Mac design. People would say, "Oh, I need this or that." I could just make it. A bitmap display is like a grid, you had a certain number of pixels. Ones and zeros, black or white, and you wrote an icon editor. You could just tap a square in that grid and turn it from black to white. Even just a tiny icon there were a lot of considerations. What is it? What does it represent? Who's it for? Where are they going to see it? What is really the heart of the thing that needs a symbol? These details cumulatively had an effect on the product. What do buttons look like? Scrollbar?

The Apple Macintosh appeared in 1984. It was based on an earlier Apple computer called Lisa, which also had a graphic interface, a mouse, and a keyboard. Lisa was aimed at the very top end of the small personal computer market. Macintosh was intended to be much more accessible.

Graphic interfaces had been around for 10 years already at the Xerox Palo Alto Research Center. In exchange for 100,000 shares of Apple stock in advance of its initial public offering, Xerox agreed to two research facility visits by Jobs and a few top Apple engineers. What Jobs saw floored him—the Xerox Alto computer featured a graphic user interface, driven by a mouse, a keyboard, and based around files, folders, windows, and a desktop metaphor. He immediately saw the mass potential. The Macintosh and Lisa projects were already under way, but he insisted they change course, and immediately embrace the graphic interface, as well as improve on what he had seen at Xerox. What was simply an icon-driven menu interface at Xerox became a direct manipulation interface at Apple, where the mouse as proxy for a human hand could grab, move, and even resize objects on screen. The Xerox mouse had three buttons. At Apple, the mouse has only ever had one. These ideas didn't originate at Apple, but Apple found a way to make them understandable to a mass public through design.

Still, at the time, the public had no idea of what a graphic user interface like this should look like. Kare was starting with a mostly blank slate, though one with considerable technical constraints. The screen was a meager 512 × 342 pixels and only black and white. Starting from the existing Apple Lisa interface, Kare developed a graphic language based in bitmaps, some as small as 16 × 16 pixel grids of black and white, to articulate the various aspects of the new computer's [↓] interface.

Driven also by Steve Jobs' interest, Apple made a central commitment to good typography in its system software and interfaces. (In his 2005 Stanford University commencement speech, Jobs attributes his interest in typography to wandering into a calligraphy class at Reed College. He then encourages the Stanford students to likewise follow their curiosity wherever it leads.) As a result, a small set of fonts were built directly into the Macintosh operating system, many of which were designed by Kare. Most consequentially she designed Chicago, the default system font used in all of Macintosh's interfaces. This type was designed to address the rigors of a one color, low-resolution bitmapped display, and to be immediately legible and clear in the context of a novel graphic interface. Here's Chicago [↓], a good bit enlarged.

The quick brown fox jumps over a lazy dog.

And here it is again [↓], in the context of the interface.

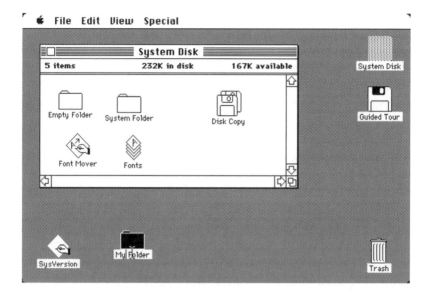

On the top left of the screen, anchored by an apple, the nested pull-down menus performed system-wide actions. Here is the Macintosh control panel [↓], a tour de force of early interface design.

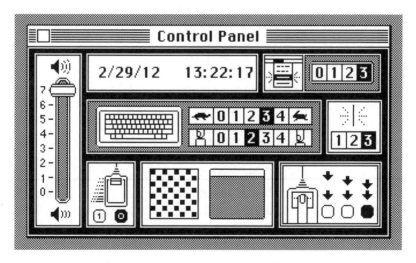

On this condensed graphic, the user adjusts what is adjustable in the behavior of the interface. So, for example volume is on the left [↖]. At the bottom right is the control for double click speed [↗], which was import-ant at the time because double clicks were an entirely new behavior and required some individual tuning. The control in the top right shows values of 0, 1, 2, 3 and this sets how many times a menu item flashed. Selecting an item from a pull-down menu was unfamiliar, so it was important that you know when you've made a selection, and perhaps some users needed more confirmation than others. The control with both a keyboard, a turtle, and a hare at the center of the panel adjusts how quickly a key starts repeating when it is held down. Time and date are set in the top middle; bottom middle are mouse speed and desktop pattern. Finally, bottom far right is the text cursor blinking rate.

Many of these settings seem strange to us now, but this gives an indication of just how new this computer interface was for its users. The engineering team identified what might need to be adjusted, but Kare, as the sole source of interface graphics at Apple, was left to invent the graphic language that could communicate these new behaviors.

Perhaps an even clearer example is the toolbox she designed in 1984 for the Macintosh image manipulation program MacPaint [↙].

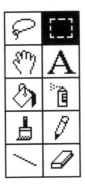

The lasso was invented to mark an irregular selection; the rectangular marquee for a regular selection. The hand moves around the image (a pan), the capital A indicates the text tool, a paint bucket fills a selected area. The spray can, paint brush, and pencil behave as expected, and for that matter, so do the line and eraser tools. In Kare's toolbar, software functions are inseparable from their icons even taking on the name of the icon (the "hand" tool, for example). This was years before Photoshop and decades before the Adobe Creative Suite, and still this toolbox is intimately familiar.

Ok, well, I'd like to play this excerpt from a San Francisco television interview with Susan Kare from this time, right around 1984.

TV host: Joining us now Susan Kare. Susan is an icon designer with the Macintosh Software Group and Jerry Manock, who is product design manager for Macintosh. We're talking, Jerry, about ergonomics on the show, how did the....

We're going to skip Jerry, as we're interested in the interface.

TV host: OK, your area, the icons, are another one of the key ergonomic aspects I suppose of using a Mac. Maybe you can run through a demonstration here, Susan, and show us how we use the icons to get from place to place. Tell us where we are right at this moment with the Mac?

Susan Kare: Well, what you see now is the image, the icon that you get when you just plug Mac in and turn it on. It prompts you with a picture of the diskette [↘].

TV host: And a question mark saying, "Where's my diskette?"

Susan Kare: Saying, "I need something." So that all you do is—it only fits in one way. So there's no way you can break it or make a mistake. You just pop it in. You get an image of a content Mac so you know that everything is OK [↘].

And you're welcomed. It's just so that the person using Mac gets information all the time visually so nothing has to be translated. A little wristwatch to tell you just wait one second [↓].

TV host: Things are happening. You've replaced the salt timer very quickly.

Susan Kare: It's moving into the '80s.

TV host: So what do we have now?

Susan Kare: So what we have now is an image on the screen of the diskette that we put in the slot, and it can be, with the mouse, it can be moved.

TV host: And it's already showing you the name of that disk.

Susan Kare: Right. And it's highlighted in the sense that it's inverted so that Mac knows that you want to do something to this diskette [↙].

Your choices of what you might want to do are listed in hidden menus that operate a little bit like window shades when you move your cursor [↙].

TV host: So let's pull down the file menus. That would tell us now what?

Susan Kare: Right. There are choices. We can find out something about this diskette, or we can just open it. Or we can eject it. But if we open it. Just say open. And immediately we get what we call a window that displays graphically and in words what is contained on the diskette, the machine [↓].

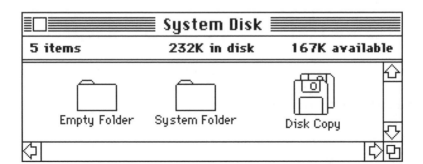

Some of the icons Kare designed were simply evolutions from the exsiting Lisa interface. For example, she upgraded Lisa's [] "wastebasket" with the slightly sleeker [] Mac trashcan:

Others took more invention, which she approached first with a pen on graph paper. The "hand" tool, for example, was tricky. Here are a few alternate versions [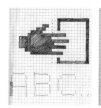] [] [] and the finished graphic []:

Others were borrowed. In a pre-release version of Macintosh system software, Steve Jobs complained there were too many apples in the interface, and charged Kare with replacing the command modifier key (at that time marked by an apple) with something else. After struggling for a while, she came up with this mark [] which turns out to also mark sights of special interest in Sweden, here [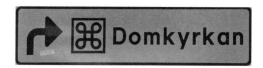] pointing toward a cathedral.

Still others were drawn from life, like this icon for Steve Jobs, buried as an Easter egg in the Macintosh system software [].

And there are others you hope not to see, like the sad Mac which tells you something is wrong [].

But the one you really didn't want to see was this one—the bomb [🗲].
It marked absolute system failure.

I'm exhausted, and I think that's a good place to stop.

Further Reading

Apple. "Apple Human Interface Guidelines (Watch OS)." Accessed June 11, 2019. https://developer.apple.com/watch/human-interface-guidelines/

Barbacetto, G., and Achille Castiglioni. *Design Interface: How Man and Machine Communicate: Olivetti Design Research by King & Miranda*. Milano: Arcadia, 1987.

Calvino, Italo. *Mr. Palomar*. 1st American ed. San Diego: Harcourt Brace Jovanovich, 1985.

Caso, Alfonso. *Calendarios, Códices y Manuscritos Antiguos (Zapotecas y Mixtecas)*. Mexico City: El Colegio Nacional, 2007.

Eco, Umberto. "Form as Social Commitment," in *The Open Work*. Cambridge, MA: Harvard University Press, 1990.

Ford, Paul. "Code: An Essay," *Bloomberg Businessweek*, June 15–June 28, 2015.

Giampietro, Rob. "I am a Handle," *Bulletins of The Serving Library #2*, http://www.servinglibrary.org/journal/2/i-am-a-handle, 2012.

Google. "Material Design." Accessed June 11, 2019. https://material.io/design/introduction/

Harwood, John. *The Interface: IBM and the Transformation of Corporate Design*, 1945–1976. Minneapolis: University of Minnesota Press, 2011.

Jespersen, James, Jane Fitz-Randolph, and John Robb. *From Sundials to Atomic Clocks: Understanding Time and Frequency*. Washington D.C.: National Bureau of Standards, U.S. Dept. of Commerce, 1977.

Keramidas, Kimon. *The Interface Experience: A User's Guide*. New York: Bard Graduate Center, 2015.

Lange, Alexandra. "What We've Learned From Dieter Rams, and What We've Ignored," *The New Yorker*, November 28, 2018.

Moggridge, Bill. *Designing Interactions*. Cambridge, MA: MIT Press, 2007.

Rawsthorne, Alice. "By Design," *Frieze*, July–August, 2015.

Reinfurt, David, and Robert Wiesenberger. *Muriel Cooper*. Cambridge, MA: MIT Press, 2017.

Stephenson, Neal. *In the Beginning... was the Command Line*. New York: Avon Books, 1999.

Tanchis, Aldo, and Bruno Munari. *Bruno Munari: Design As Art*. Cambridge, MA: MIT Press, 1987.

http://www.i-n-t-e-r-f-a-c-e.org

Author Acknowledgments

This book was assembled over eight years of teaching in the Program in Visual Arts at the Lewis Center for the Arts, Princeton University. It was developed in and for class lectures, so I must first thank all the students who sat through these. In particular, graphic design students Kara Bressler, Ben Denzer, Nazlı Ercan, Lily Healey, Eric Li, Neeta Patel, Matt Rogers, Nathan Tyrell, Simon Wu, and Jonathan Zong each helped steer the *new* program through dialogue, concern, and criticism.

The Program in Visual Arts was fundamental. Its former director, Joe Scanlan, first invited me to introduce graphic design at Princeton and then helped it to grow. Its current director, Martha Friedman, has since tirelessly supported it. A series of inspiring instructors have developed and taught these courses, including Danielle Aubert, Alice Chung, Francesca Grassi, Peter Kazantsev, and David Sellers.

For project support, thank you to the Graham Foundation for Advanced Studies in the Fine Arts, Lewis Center for the Arts at Princeton University, and the Barr Ferree Foundation Fund for Publications, Department of Art and Archaeology, Princeton University.

Much of this material was fostered by 10 years of collaboration with Stuart Bertolotti-Bailey as Dexter Sinister, and versions of some texts appeared in either *Dot Dot Dot* (edited by Bertolotti-Bailey) or *Bulletins of the Serving Library* (edited by Bertolotti-Bailey, Francesca Bertolotti-Bailey, Angie Keefer, and Vincenzo Latronico). Paul Elliman at Yale University School of Art taught me what I know about teaching by generously teaching very little.

Thank you to editor Eugenia Bell who made sense of my speech in print and to designer Siiri Tännler who gave it graceful form. Finally, thank you to Inventory Press—Shannon Harvey and Adam Michaels—who both identified the potential and conspired to make it happen in an expansive spirit that fits the original intent.

—David Reinfurt, New York, July 2019

Publisher Acknowledgments

Our day-to-day at IN-FO.CO and Inventory Press is spent designing, editing, and publishing, spanning a variety of configurations and scenarios. It's a rare pleasure for graphic design to be the direct subject of our work, and we are grateful to be able to play a role in initiating and bringing this book to fruition—an outcome that would have been impossible without the committed support of many others.

For the three-day lecture in Los Angeles, we are grateful to Dion Neutra for allowing full access to the former Neutra Architects office; Kali Nikitas, Tanya Rubbak, and Otis College of Art and Design for supporting the event and mobilizing student interest; Lewis Center for the Arts at Princeton University for supporting the exhibition; Ross Harris for video documentation; Eric Li from O-R-G for logistical support; and Gloria Kondrup and the Hoffmitz Milken Center for Typography for a follow-up event at ArtCenter. Many thanks to everyone who attended the lectures, whether for a short drop-in or an extended stay, all contributing to a memorable few days.

For this book, our deepest gratitude to Eugenia Bell for editing and Siiri Tännler for design. Thank you to Ellen Lupton for her foreword; the Graham Foundation for Advanced Studies in the Fine Arts for its generous support; Andrew Blauvelt and Zoë Ryan for early encouragement; and Michael Sakkali at die Keure for support. Thank you to our co-publisher D.A.P., especially Sharon Helgason Gallagher and Elisa Nadel, for helping make this project possible.

And for direct and indirect support and camaraderie, we would like to thank everyone who has worked with us at IN-FO.CO and IP during this time, including Hayden Anderson, Adam Bandler, Nolan Boomer, Jeremiah Chiu, Hana Cohn, Matteo Cossu, Lauren Gideonse, Ella Gold, Dani Grossman, Levi Murphy, Yuri Sakakibara, Parker Sprout, and Orly Vermes.

And finally, thank you to David Reinfurt, for many years of inspiration and for his willingness to speak this book into the present form.

—Adam Michaels & Shannon Harvey, Los Angeles, July 2019

A *New* Program for Graphic Design
is published by
Inventory Press, LLC
2305 Hyperion Ave
Los Angeles, CA 90027
inventorypress.com
&
D.A.P./Distributed Art Publishers
75 Broad Street, Suite 630
New York, NY 10004
artbook.com

Editors: Eugenia Bell, Adam Michaels
Design: IN-FO.CO (Adam Michaels,
Shannon Harvey, Siiri Tännler)

Audio transcription: Hayden Anderson
Image permissions: Orly Vermes

Printed and bound in Belgium by die Keure

ISBN: 978-1-941753-21-7

LCCN: 2019950468

Distributed by
ARTBOOK | D.A.P.
75 Broad Street, Suite 630
New York, NY 10004
artbook.com

This book has been generously
supported by the Graham Foundation
for Advanced Studies in the Fine
Arts, and is made possible in part by
the Barr Ferree Foundation Fund
for Publications, Department of Art
and Archaeology, Princeton University
and by Lewis Center for the Arts,
Princeton University.

Notes on the Type

Gerstner-Programm
Originally designed by Karl Gerstner
between 1964–67 for then current
phototype technology as a systemized
interpretation of late 19th-century
metal type Akzidenz-Grotesk, and more
recently adapted as a digital type family
by Stephan Müller, released by Forgotten
Shapes in 2018.

Menlo
Designed by Jim Lyles for release
as an Apple system font in 2009,
Menlo is based on the Open Source
font Bitstream Vera, which is in
turn based on Biststream Prima, and
also relates to the public domain
font Deja Vu.